Women's Leadership and Participation

Praise for the book ...

'The absence of women's voices in decisions which affect their lives is not only a problem for women but is usually a sign of unjust power relations that exclude many men as well. The eight case studies in this book drawn from around the world give rich, concrete insights into strategies for change in such situations – ones which effectively build women's leadership and participation in economic, social and political spheres. They illustrate how women are often at the forefront of change, not just to raise their own voices, but in so doing to create more just and democratic societies for others as well.'

John Gaventa, Professor, Participation, Power and
Social Change team, Institute of Development Studies

'As someone who has spent 20 years on Women's Leadership and Participation right around the world I very much welcome this new Oxfam Publication. Its vivid case studies show how women can successfully raise their voices at local, national and international levels, essential for poverty alleviation and overcoming gender inequality. Excellent reading for civil servants in aid departments, NGOs, IGOs such as the UN, OECD, OSCE, World Bank – and everyone working for a better, saner and fairer world.'

Lesley Abdela, Senior Partner, Eyecatcher/Shevolution

'This collection of innovations in supporting women's engagement in political competition provides inspiring examples of how to accelerate the much-anticipated positive effects of increasing the numbers of women in politics. Under the right conditions, more women in public office do deliver better governance for all. This volume provides us with inspiring guidance for building gender equality into political life.'

Anne Marie Goetz, Chief Advisor, Governance Peace and Security,
UNIFEM

Women's Leadership and Participation
Case studies on learning for action

Edited by Joanna Hoare and Fiona Gell

Published by Practical Action Publishing Ltd in association with Oxfam GB.

Practical Action Publishing Ltd
Schumacher Centre for Technology and Development
Bourton on Dunsmore, Rugby,
Warwickshire, CV23 9QZ, UK
www.practicalactionpublishing.org

ISBN 978 1 85339 696 0

© Oxfam GB, 2009

Since 1974, Practical Action Publishing (formerly Intermediate Technology
Publications and ITDG Publishing) has published and disseminated books and
information in support of international development work throughout the world.
Practical Action Publishing Ltd (Company Reg. No. 1159018) is the wholly owned
publishing company of Practical Action. Practical Action Publishing trades only
in support of its parent charity objectives and any profits are covenanted back to
Practical Action (Charity Reg. No. 247257, Group VAT Registration No. 880 9924 76).

Oxfam is a registered charity in England and Wales (no 202918) and Scotland
(SCO 039042). Oxfam GB is a member of Oxfam International.

Oxfam GB,
Oxfam House, John Smith Drive,
Oxford, OX4 2JY, UK
www.oxfam.org.uk

Cover photo: Women piloting the Women's Coastal Zone project arrive from their
exposure visit to a marine sanctuary site in Pangasinan province, Philippines.
Credit: Gaynor Tanyang 2007
Indexed by Andrea Palmer
Typeset by S.J.I. Services
Printed by Hobbs The Printers Ltd
Printed on FSC 100% post-consumer waste recycled paper.

Contents

Boxes and figures

Boxes

Figures

Acknowledgements

Joanna Hoare and Fiona Gell co-edited this book. Joanna worked for Oxfam's Publishing and Programme Policy teams between January 2006 and March 2008, including a year-long stint as acting editor on *Gender & Development*. She is currently working on a PhD in Development Studies at the School of Oriental and African Studies, University of London, and also works as a freelance editor and writer on gender and development issues.

Fiona is a gender and development specialist who has worked for Oxfam GB for many years, most recently as a Global Gender Advisor. Her main areas of focus and interest have included gender in humanitarian work, women and leadership, and gender and organizational change.

Katie Allan project managed this book. She is an editorial project manager at Oxfam GB, working on a wide range of campaigns, policy, and humanitarian publications.

The **Advisory Group** for this project included the following Oxfam GB staff: Nkechi Eke Nwankwo, Alexandra Pura, Cecilia Millan, Jon Horsley, Jo Rowlands, and Sarah Totterdell. Mike Parkinson, Audrey Bronstein, and Sam Bickersteth commented on the text. Ines Smyth has been very involved in the recent development of Oxfam GB's programming on women's participation and leadership which produced much of the analysis underpinning this publication. Nicholas Pialek supported the initial stages of conceptualizing the project. Caroline Sweetman provided support and advice on chapters. And Othman Mahmoud provided management oversight. Many thanks to all of these people whose contributions have been vital to the production of this book.

CHAPTER 1
Women's leadership and participation: overview

Joanna Hoare and Fiona Gell

Contributors: Caroline Sweetman, Ines Smyth, and Anna Coates

Introduction

Why support women's participation and leadership?

Throughout both the developing and the developed world, women carry a disproportionately high burden of poverty. This poverty is experienced not just as material deprivation, but also as marginalization, which means that those living in poverty often have no, or little opportunity to influence the political, economic, and social processes and institutions which control and shape their lives and keep them trapped in a cycle of poverty.

For poor women, this experience of marginalization is effectively doubled: not only do they belong to communities that exist 'on the edges of society', but they are also often denied a voice *within* the states, markets, communities, and households in which they live, dominated as they are by men and male interests. This lack of voice functions as a critical factor in the maintenance of gender inequality and poverty, effectively blocking women's access to decision-making and agenda-setting processes, and beyond that, opportunities for leading these processes. This situation contributes to an invisibility of women as public actors and constitutes a negation of their rights to equal participation. It also perpetuates a decision-making process which is less likely to represent women's interests than a more representative system and which, therefore, possesses neither the vision nor the motivation to challenge or change unequal gender relations in society.

Women's equal participation and leadership in decision-making processes at every level and in every sector is therefore fundamental to attempts to eliminate gender-based poverty. In order to challenge the unequal and ultimately unsustainable economic and social systems in which we live, and to secure the essential resources they need for dignified and rewarding lives, it has been argued that women need 'to be visible politically *as women* and be empowered to act in that capacity, because...they...have needs and attitudes on vital issues which differ from those of men'.[1] Women's presence in significant numbers in elected bodies and in economic institutions can result in more equitable policy outcomes because it is likely to encourage policy makers to give more attention to issues affecting women, such as equal pay, better conditions of employment, child-care, violence against women, and unpaid labour.[2] And economic policies are also more likely to acknowledge the value of unpaid caring work (most of which is done by women) as an economic asset to be maintained and developed.

For instance, in Norway, women members of Parliament brought about the 'politics of care', which obligates the state to increase publicly sponsored child-care services, extend parental leave and flexible working, and improve pension rights for carers.[3] In South Africa, women parliamentarians have led the world in the process of introducing gender budgeting to analyse state spending from a gender perspective and allocate resources to women's needs.[4] While having more women in leadership positions does not guarantee women's concerns will be on the agenda, there is evidence that once a critical mass of women – over one-third – is in power, their shared interests *as women* start to come to the fore, as these two examples illustrate.[5]

Not only is women's participation and leadership an essential prerequisite for poverty alleviation and tackling gender inequality, it is also a basic human right. International human-rights treaties and conventions such as the Convention on the Elimination of All Forms of Discrimination Against Women (CEDAW),[6] the Beijing Platform for Action,[7] and the third Millennium Development Goal on gender equality, recognize that women have the right to participate equally with men at all levels and in all aspects of public life and decision-making, whether it is deciding how the household income is spent or determining how the country is run, and such conventions commit signatories to realizing this goal.

Despite these commitments to promoting gender equality in formal structures of representation and decision-making, women continue to be under-represented in all areas of decision-making and face significant barriers to their full and equal participation in the structures and institutions that govern, and directly affect, their lives.

Why women's participation and leadership is critical to Oxfam GB's work

As a rights-based humanitarian, development, and campaigning organization which works with others to overcome poverty and suffering, Oxfam GB has, for many years, sought to ensure that women's right to equal participation in the design and delivery of programmes is respected, so that they have greater influence over decisions affecting their lives. Increasingly there is a drive to go beyond this and support women's leadership of the institutions and processes that perpetuate the gendered inequalities of wealth and power that reinforce the denial of women's rights, giving particular support and encouragement to transformative leadership that seeks explicitly to challenge those inequalities.

This book documents learning from programmes that Oxfam GB and its partners have been supporting around the world. Case studies from the Philippines, Israel, and the UK detail projects which have sought to nurture and draw attention to women's participation and leadership in the economic sphere, through supporting their activities in civil-society organizations. Four chapters – from Sierra Leone, Honduras, Cambodia, and Haiti – describe programme work to encourage women's political participation in formal government structures. Finally, the case study from Chile makes the important link between increasing women's visibility in the economic and social sectors, and engaging in advocacy to promote women's employment rights at the political level.

Activities described here have taken place at all levels, from working with marginalized women to identify, articulate, and lobby on community-level issues of concern in the UK, to supporting elected representatives and ministers to incorporate a gender and poverty analysis into their work at senior government levels in Sierra Leone, Honduras, and Haiti. In all these case studies, no matter the level at which activities are taking place, what emerges strongly is the need to challenge actively the stereotypes, attitudes, and beliefs that continue to limit women's opportunities to realize their potential as active citizens and leaders. While all women are affected by these stereotypes, those living in poverty face further prejudice not just because of their gender identity, but also because of their class (or caste) identity, levels of education, and often racial or ethnic identity as well, all of which intersect to render them 'unfit' for positions of leadership and influence, in the eyes of powerful elites. These prejudices need to be challenged and addressed at every level, including by those women who do succeed in attaining formal positions of power and influence, and by male leaders. It is not enough just to 'get women into power'; once there, they need to be supported and encouraged to act in the best interests of *all* women, to be held accountable to this responsibility, and to influence their male peers to do the same.

This is not an arena of 'quick fixes' and instant impact, but one where change is happening gradually, as women leaders and would-be leaders are nurtured and supported to engage with and participate in decision-making processes in a way that challenges inequalities and injustice. Reflecting this, many of the programmes featured here are as yet unable to provide concrete examples of how women's increased participation and leadership have brought about positive changes for women living in poverty and marginalization, beyond the very local level (in the case studies from Israel and Cambodia, for instance). That said, we feel that these case studies present some useful examples of 'work in progress' towards enabling the active participation of women from all backgrounds in decision-making structures, and towards strengthening transformative and progressive leadership, that will, in the future, bring about real and positive change for women living in poverty and marginalization.

A snapshot of women's participation and leadership in the world today

Economic institutions

In the field of economics and finance, women remain sorely under-represented in decision-making in institutions at local, national, and international levels. At government level, only 14 per cent of finance ministers are female (28 across 193 countries).[8] International institutions, which shape economic and social policy in developing countries, have few women leaders. For example, at the World Bank and International Monetary Fund, women comprise around 20 per cent of leadership staff, and under 10 per cent of governors.[9] And women are woefully absent at the top levels of business – just 25 out of the top 1000 multinational corporations are run by women.[10] So the increasing role of the private sector in development is not showing promising signs of advancing women's empowerment.

At the household and community levels, despite women moving into many economic fields which were once male-dominated, the gender division of labour is still very real both within the home and outside it. Within the household, women carry the overwhelming burden of unpaid reproductive labour and caring work, which affects their ability to be active outside the home, and to influence economic decisions within it. In many poor rural households, women's role in agricultural production and processing often goes unrecognized or undervalued. And if women also work outside the home, they often find themselves in low-status, informal-sector jobs with few benefits and little protection. Even in the formal sector, women still earn considerably less than men. While women make up nearly 40 per cent of the global paid workforce, they earn only 26 per cent of the world's income.[11] With little or no voice in the organizations and institutions which regulate or control the economic sector, the status of women will remain unchallenged.

On the positive side, women's income, and their career options in comparison to men's, have increased significantly over the past few decades, and they have shown spectacular success in running their own businesses across the world. But despite this, women are seldom found as managers, owners, and entrepreneurs in enterprises.

Even trade unions, co-operatives, and other producer associations, which are meant to uphold and represent the rights of *all* workers, often have few women in positions of power (unless they are dedicated women's co-operatives). Trade unions in particular are very male-dominated, with the result that the particular needs and priorities of women workers are often ignored. The types of work that women engage in, and the frequent precariousness of their employment situations, may also make it very difficult for them to obtain support from, and influence the policies of, traditional trade unions.

Political institutions

In almost all countries, women have now won the right to vote. Yet there are still scandalously few women in positions of political leadership. Globally, just 17.4 per cent of national political representatives are female, and only 15 out of 193 countries worldwide have achieved 30 per cent women in national governments.[12] In addition, globally, just 3.5 per cent of senior ministerial positions are held by women, meaning that at the top levels of government, women currently have little opportunity to shape policy.[13] Lower down, in the regional and sub-regional government institutions which often play an important role in determining access to essential services and resources, women remain conspicuous by their absence. Women coming from poor backgrounds, or belonging to ethnic or other minority groups (based for instance on their sexual identity, (dis)ability, or HIV status) are particularly under-represented in formal political structures.

However, there are signs of improvement. Since 1995, the average proportion of women in national assemblies has almost doubled. There has been considerable progress in some parts of Africa. Six African countries now have better profiles for women's representation than the Europe/OSCE (Organization for Security and Co-operation in Europe) countries (excluding the Scandinavian countries).[14] The recent arrival to power of women heads of state such as Ellen Johnson-Sirleaf in Liberia and Michelle Bachelet in Chile also indicates growing acceptance of the legitimacy of women leaders. Bachelet's election in particular provides hope, given that she campaigned on an openly pro-gender equality and women's rights agenda. This agenda is now being transformed into policy decisions strengthening the rights of women in Chile, such as increasing child-care provision for low-income mothers, and legislation to allow access to emergency contraception.

Civil-society institutions

Because of women's historic lack of presence in formal government and the structural barriers they face in entering the political sphere, many women have sought leadership positions within civil-society organizations, as a means of finding alternative ways to forge the changes and obtain the responses they seek.[15] In an example from Israel and the Occupied Palestinian Territories included here, poor Israeli-Arab women who are marginalized within their own communities, as well as within Israeli society more generally, have been able to secure influence through their activism within a civil-society organization campaigning on rights for the unemployed.

However, even in NGOs and community-based organizations which claim to represent 'the community', women are much less likely to be leaders than men, and women's shared interests are less likely to be on the agenda. Community-based organizations may also end up being dominated by the interests of more powerful, wealthy members of the community, again marginalizing poorer women's priorities and experiences. Women have founded their own organizations in response to this, yet these are often sidelined from policy processes involving civil-society organizations, and again, may reflect the interests of women who are already in relative positions of influence and power, rather than those lower down the social scale.

Barriers to women's participation and leadership, and strategies to overcome them

There are many factors which constrain women's ability to participate on an equal footing with men and to take up positions of leadership, regardless of whether they are poor or not, but these factors always impact hardest on poor women. Institutional gender bias represents a challenge to all women seeking equal participation and competing for leadership positions, as does the way that political and economic systems are organized. Scepticism and mistrust of women's ability to lead, and the stereotypes and prejudices about their role in society and their lack of suitability for leadership roles and decision-making, are other major challenges for all women.

Women living in poverty face a range of additional barriers. Lack of education and low levels of literacy make access to information difficult and commonly undermine the confidence and skills needed to enter public life whether at village, community, local, or national level. Lack of financial resources restrict poor women's opportunities and confidence to risk competing for, and maintaining, leadership positions, as well as not allowing them to purchase caring support for dependants, which is often crucial to enable them to combine active public and family lives. Women are also less likely than men to have the networks, contacts, and social and professional experience expected of public leaders. Women living in poverty carry the overwhelming burden of reproductive labour within families; in many contexts, this includes collecting fuel and water, and cultivating subsistence crops to feed their families. This means that time is a critical resource. For poor women, participating in public decision-making beyond their immediate needs for survival may seem like an impossible extra burden. Restrictions on women's mobility, be they cultural, legal, or the result of women's own fears of encountering violence and harassment if they leave the safety of their own communities, may make travelling to take part in meetings or forums very difficult. This also limits campaigning opportunities for women seeking election to formal positions of power. In addition, women living in poverty are subject to particular gender-related risks and vulnerabilities caused by factors such as HIV, disability, and gender-based violence, all of which compound their inability to participate on an equal footing with men.

Carrying out 'gender audits' of one kind or another – for instance, research into how a particular issue or policy is impacting on women's well-being, as detailed in the Philippines case study (relating to trade liberalization), or a participatory needs assessment, as undertaken by Oxfam GB's partner

Sawt el-Amel in Israel (to determine how women were being affected by the Wisconsin Plan, a new 'welfare to work' programme) – are an important way of assessing what factors are limiting women's opportunities for participation in a particular context, in order to find ways of challenging and overcoming those limitations.

In broad terms there are three areas which need to be tackled:

- overcoming structural barriers;
- encouraging and supporting women to take up leadership roles or participate in decision-making on an equal footing with men;
- supporting women and men to carry out leadership roles which challenge inequalities of wealth and power and recognize and promote women's rights.

These will now be examined in greater depth, drawing examples from the case studies included in this book.

Overcoming the structural barriers to women's participation and leadership

Legislative reform

In the political sphere, the way elections are organized and run, especially in the selection of candidates, presents women with particular problems, whether this is getting selected for a constituency-based election or appearing on a party list of candidates. Lack of knowledge, lack of access to patronage networks, lack of financial support, and active or perceived prejudice against women candidates all act as structural barriers to women participating in elections for public office at all levels of representation. For instance, in Sierra Leone, women candidates reported that political parties would often remove women from candidate lists at the last minute, replacing them with male candidates who, they felt, were more likely to win the seat.

In light of this, electoral reform can provide new opportunities for women seeking to become leaders in the political arena. The implementation of quotas and reservation of seats have been the key instruments in increasing women's political representation, and over 40 countries have adopted quota[16] laws to regulate the selection or election of women to political office. In several of the examples included in this book – Sierra Leone, Haiti, Honduras – lobbying for the implementation or extension of quotas for women candidates has formed a central part of the programme's long-term work on women's participation and leadership, as has educating women voters about legislative changes, to encourage them to realize their right to participate in elections. However, women's interests as a collective group have not necessarily been advanced by quotas, as women who do succeed in reaching leadership roles may be unaware of the need (or be unwilling) to champion women's rights and influence their male colleagues to do the same. Because of this, if used in isolation or understood as being sufficient to bring about women's wider equality, quotas are vulnerable to political manipulation and have limited transformative power.[17] And if the political will to implement quotas is lacking, and no mechanisms exist to enforce compliance, political parties and state structures may simply ignore them, as the example from Honduras illustrates.

Policies of decentralization have been of particular significance in increasing women's representation at the local level. These give local and regional governments (rather than central government) the power to make decisions about local services, such as health, education, and sanitation. Because it is often easier for women to get elected at local level than at national level, decentralization can give women real influence over decisions which will have a direct impact on the lives of members of their communities. In recognition of this, the introduction of decentralization policies in Cambodia and Sierra Leone prompted Oxfam GB and its partners to give support to women standing for election to local government.

Increasing visibility in the economic sector

Women's under-representation in leadership roles in the economic sphere contributes to: the undervaluing and lack of recognition of their contribution to the paid and unpaid economy; working conditions and production processes that do not meet their needs; lack of access to and control of economic resources; and their concentration at the lower end of the economic value chain, meaning they enjoy lower economic returns.

An important first step in strengthening women's opportunities to participate in decision-making and to attain leadership positions in the economic sector is making their contributions to that sector visible. Recognizing this, in both the Philippines and in Chile, Oxfam GB and its partners worked to highlight women's vital contributions to the fishing sector and to the agricultural export sector respectively. In the Philippines, 'gender audits' helped to identify what contributions women are making to the fishing industry as a whole, and illuminate how the way in which worker organizations operate was making it difficult for women to participate actively. This highlighted the need for the creation of more inclusive management structures and for leadership training to enable women to participate more effectively in them. In Chile, Oxfam GB has facilitated links between women's rights organizations, trade unions, and mainstream civil-society organizations, as well as supporting a network of women agricultural workers to represent and lobby on behalf of women workers. This has led to a greater awareness of women's presence in the agricultural export industry, and of the vulnerability and exploitation that women workers experience, which in turn has meant that these alliances have lobbied effectively for changes in national level legislation to protect women workers' rights.

In Israel, the introduction of the Wisconsin Plan, an unpopular 'welfare to work' programme, prompted women from the Arab minority to act, on the grounds that the programme had a negative impact on women, was exploitative, and put the welfare of families in jeopardy. For many women, this was the first time that they had taken part in any kind of public activity. Doing so has unleashed their enormous potential for leadership and activism, as well as making them visible in public as a collective group. This was recognized by Oxfam GB's partner organization Sawt el-Amel, and for the first time, women are now integrated into the organization's leadership structure.

Changing attitudes to women's leadership and participation

Traditional attitudes and beliefs about women's role in society continue to prejudice both men's and women's preconceptions regarding women's ability to participate fully in public life. These attitudes include stereotypes about women being dependent, unskilled, and not suitable for institutional leadership and strategic decision-making. People may even question the 'morality' of women seeking leadership positions. In Sierra Leone, many women candidates reported experiencing hostility from female voters in particular, who told them to 'go back home where they belong'. Elsewhere, in many conservative contexts women are actively prohibited from engagement in activities outside the home.

Working with women in the fishing industry in the Philippines, Oxfam GB and its partners found that a major obstacle to women's active participation and leadership was the women's own acceptance of existing gender roles and relations. In response to this, part of Oxfam GB's work has consisted not only of encouraging women in the fishing industry to recognize that they have the right to be leaders, but also encouraging women to reconsider their gendered perceptions about 'what makes a good leader'. In the UK, women participating in training to encourage economic and political participation and empowerment did not really have any sense of shared solidarity as women. It was only through meeting women from other parts of the country, and identifying and discussing common problems that they faced, that the participants came to realize that in fact, as women, they did face many of the same issues, and that many of these were the result of gender inequality, and stereotypes regarding acceptable masculine and feminine behaviour. These examples underline how important it is to remember that any work in this field must include activities that challenge women's own perceptions about their suitability for leadership.

Working to encourage men to be more receptive to the idea of women occupying positions of power is also critical in challenging the inequality and discrimination that women face. In Sierra Leone, as well as providing gender training to male politicians and leaders, Oxfam GB's partner the 50/50 Group is seeking to identify male 'champions' in positions of authority, who will be prepared to speak out in support of women's right to political leadership and participation. Such champions are crucial, the 50/50 Group argue, in changing other men's attitudes, as well as encouraging those men who reject male dominance and support more equal participation and leadership in development processes to speak out.

It is also true that 'actions speak louder than words'. In the Arab communities in Israel affected by the unpopular Wisconsin Plan, women have come to lead resistance to the Plan. Initially, some men objected to their wives and sisters participating in public protests. But now that the men in these communities have seen the benefits that the women's activism and leadership is bringing, most are supportive, and are happy to follow women's leadership in this campaign. In a society which is very traditional with regards to gender roles, and where women's mobility and activity is tightly controlled by male relatives, this represents a significant shift in gender power relations.

Dealing with constraints on women's time and mobility

Among the many practical barriers facing women who wish to take a more active role in the political, economic, and civil-society sectors is lack of time. There is a strong male bias in the work culture of many institutions, many of which favour leaders who have a traditional 'male' role in family life over those who carry out unpaid caring work. This places women at a distinct disadvantage, given the fact that everywhere, women are expected to undertake the bulk of domestic and child-care work, often in addition to paid work outside the home; younger married women in particular are likely to experience 'time poverty', given that they are often responsible not just for looking after their own children and husbands, but also members of their husband's extended family. In many contexts, these caring responsibilities will extend to collecting fuel and water, and growing food to feed their families.

Lack of control over if or when to have children also makes it difficult for women to plan their participation in leadership contests or elections, underlining how important reproductive rights are to enabling women to participate and lead. Those women who have become successful as leaders have often been able to do so because they have not had dependants to care for, are wealthy enough to be able to buy in care and other domestic help, or have been able to plan when to have their children, and how many to have. In the long term, attitudes need to change, and household labour needs to be more equally divided among all household members, men included. But in the short term, many of the programmes described in these case studies made sure that leadership training did not add to women's already considerable workload. In the Philippines and in Honduras, women receiving leadership training were offered free child-care, while in the UK, training was scheduled to fit around the school day, and in a way that meant the participants did not lose access to state benefits.

Limits on women's mobility are also a significant barrier to full participation, and to attaining positions of leadership. In many instances, these limitations are cultural. For instance, in the Arab community in Israel, it is generally not considered acceptable for women to be active outside the home, making women's involvement in the public campaign against the Wisconsin Plan there particularly significant. But in other contexts, these limitations may be practical and economic, often relating to the need to care for young children and the inability to pay for transport and/or child-care costs. They may also be the result of women's own lack of self-confidence and experience of travelling on their own, or speaking in public. In Honduras, Oxfam GB's partners provided women from poor, rural communities with free transport to attend meetings with candidates standing for election so that they could actively participate in democratic processes, as well as providing free, on-site child-care to rural indigenous women who were attending leadership training at an 'advocacy school'. In the UK, as well as paying for transport and accommodation to enable women to attend lobbying meetings in London, Oxfam GB's partners ensured that the women travelled and attended meetings in pairs, so that they would not feel isolated.

Addressing inequalities of wealth and power

At every level, from the household to national government, unequal power relations impact on women's ability to participate fully in public life, and to attain positions of leadership. There are many ways that this power inequality is maintained, for example through: the use (or threat) of violence against women; restrictions on women's activities, dress, or movement which are sanctioned by culture or religion; gender stereotyping that presents women's unequal place in society as 'natural' and 'normal'; and patronage systems and networks that are dominated by men and male interests.

In the Philippines, Oxfam GB's partner organization Developers found that encouraging women participants to analyse and discuss their own experiences of violence within the family led to their realizing the extent to which violence impacts more generally on women's abilities to participate in decision-making processes outside the home. Participants then went on to raise awareness of violence against women within their community, and to lobby for local development plans to address gender-based violence.

Lack of funding is identified as an important obstacle in many of the case studies dealing with women's political leadership. This is not surprising, given the extent to which poverty disproportionately affects women everywhere, resulting from, as well as contributing to, their unequal status in society; but it may also result from women failing to gain full support from the political parties for which they are standing. In Sierra Leone, women who had stood for election in the 2004 local elections said that the small grants given to them by the 50/50 Group, Oxfam GB's partner, had made an enormous difference in terms of enabling them to pay for travel and other expenses during their campaigning. But allocating funding in this way is not ideal, not least because it could be seen as compromising the neutrality of projects designed to support women candidates, and because it is only ever a short-term solution to the problem. Recognizing this, the 50/50 Group is also campaigning to reduce the current financial requirements for standing for election. In Honduras, Oxfam GB's partner organizations are pressing for a reduction in the campaign period, again because this would cut down on the amount of money that women candidates would have to spend on campaigning. Ultimately, of course, the only sustainable solution will be an improvement in the economic status of all women.

Encouraging and supporting women to take up, and be effective in, leadership roles

Providing targeted training to women who want to assume positions of leadership is one way of enabling more women to influence decision-making processes. Several of the chapters in this collection give examples of women wishing to stand for election being provided with training that included, according to context, leadership and campaign skills, knowledge of political systems and structures, and how to develop and propose agendas that uphold women's rights. Activities also included legal-rights education or voter awareness-raising around elections, mobilizing women to vote in elections and to hold elected representatives to account. Such campaigns are often vital in contexts where poor women in particular may have little awareness of their rights as voters and as citizens. Due to lack of literacy skills and their exclusion from channels of information, they may not have any way of finding out about these rights for themselves. For instance, some of the women community leaders who took part in training in Sierra Leone were not even aware that they had the right to *vote,* let alone stand for election.

An important challenge for organizations such as Oxfam GB or its partners is how this support can be delivered in as impartial a way as is possible, in order to maintain a distinction between supporting an increase in women's participation in political and economic institutions and avoiding a perception that the programme supports particular political interests. Another challenge is making sure that women from a diverse range of backgrounds – ethnicity, age, level of education, (dis)ability, socio-economic status – are included in training activities. This is something which has been achieved with varying levels of success in these programmes.

While training and support is important for women as they seek to attain positions of power, all too often, once they have been elected, or have attained a position of leadership, women find that they are left to 'fend for themselves' in what can be a very hostile environment. In the Women In Leadership Project (WIL), the first stage of Oxfam GB and the 50/50 Group's work on promoting women's political participation and leadership in Sierra Leone, emphasis was placed on preparing women (most of whom came from poor backgrounds and had no experience of formal leadership positions) for election. Once elected, many women councillors felt overwhelmed by and ill-equipped for the duties that they were now expected to undertake, often as a result of poor literacy skills, particularly when it came to working in English. So in the second stage of this work, the Promoting A Culture of Equal Representation (PACER) project, ongoing mentoring support is being offered to women councillors and members of Parliament, to help them to be more effective in their roles.

In Haiti, as well as supporting women standing for election, Oxfam GB's partner Fanm Yo La provides ongoing training to women councillors, senators, and deputies. In addition, the 'Women in Politics School' aims to motivate local women to enter politics and take up leadership roles. In Cambodia, Oxfam GB's partner Women For Prosperity has established regular Female Councillor Forums (FCFs), where women councillors can gain experience of speaking in public in a supportive environment, and learn from other councillors who have dealt with discrimination and other problems successfully. The benefits of this are tangible, with participants reporting that they now feel comfortable contributing to council debates, standing up to discrimination, and assuming extra responsibilities, such as leading committees.

Oxfam GB's work in the UK does not centre on preparing women for formal positions of leadership, but rather on encouraging women living in poverty to engage with the institutions that make decisions which impact on their lives. Central to this is building women's confidence, and encouraging them to recognize that they have the right to challenge situations and decisions which they think are unfair, or which will have a negative impact. But another important aspect of this work has been preparing those in positions of power so that they are ready to really listen to what the women have to say, in order to make such exchanges as worthwhile as possible for both sides.

Beyond developing women's capacities to lead, there is a need to transform models of leadership development so that they become more gender responsive, and include issues such as participatory governance and inclusive dialogue, as exemplified by the Philippines case study. This is a relatively new area of thinking that has enormous potential for strengthening leadership on women's rights.

Supporting women and men to carry out leadership roles which recognize and promote women's rights

If increasing the profile of women in leadership roles is to be successful as a means of benefiting women living in poverty, this must be linked to a broader process of promoting women's rights and initiatives to combat poverty. In several of the case studies, increasing numbers of women in positions of power has had a direct, beneficial impact on the welfare of women living in poverty at the local level. In Cambodia, for instance, women councillors elected in local elections following the introduction of decentralization have worked to provide targeted assistance to the poorest and most marginalized members of their communities, such as those affected by HIV.

But it is important to recognize that not all formal mechanisms to increase the profile of women automatically have this outcome. For instance, in the Honduras case study, electoral reform led to more women being elected, but many of these new congresswomen come from religious, conservative backgrounds, and are members of the country's economic and cultural elite. They have been responsible for sponsoring regressive legislation that will limit women's rights and opportunities to advance gender equality, such as a ban on gender-sensitive sex education in schools. Women in formal positions of power will not necessarily act in the interests of other women, or of poor people or other marginalized groups. In addition, it is wrong to assume that all progressive women politicians will automatically be 'gender aware', and will incorporate women's rights and gender-equality issues into their agendas in a meaningful way.

In response to this, Oxfam GB's partners' work in Honduras since the elections has included building alliances between those congresswomen who are keen to promote women's rights and gender equality, and women's rights organizations. Both sides have benefited, with the organizations able to lobby these politicians directly, and the politicians receiving the information and ideas that they need, in order to be able to push for legislation within congress that advances gender equality and women's rights. Elsewhere, in Haiti, Sierra Leone, and Cambodia, women politicians elected to office have received training to help them identify key inequality issues affecting their constituents.

Another approach aimed at encouraging progressive candidates to integrate gender and poverty alleviation into their agendas has been the adoption of local 'pacts', or 'protocols'. In Haiti and Honduras, Oxfam GB's partner organizations facilitated meetings between voters and female and male candidates, where the former had a chance to voice their concerns and demands. Representatives from women's rights organizations were also invited to attend. At the end of the meetings, candidates formally signed a pact (in Honduras), or protocol (in Haiti), in which they pledged to be accountable to their electorate, to address the priorities identified by their constituents in the event of being elected, and to promote women's rights and gender equality.

Conclusion

Programmes aimed at strengthening women's leadership and participation will have limited impact unless the structures that uphold gender inequality, and other forms of inequality, begin to change. In addition to projects directly supporting women to participate actively in the economic, political, and civil-society sectors, many of the programmes described in these case studies have sought to challenge: unrepresentative governance and electoral systems that are not accountable to voters; organizational structures that reinforce male control and influence; and the economic discrimination that women face. For such challenges to be successful, men must be brought on board at all levels to accept the idea of women occupying positions of power, to support women in attaining and carrying out effective leadership that challenges all forms of inequality, and to work with women to develop collective agendas for upholding women's rights.

Some of the principles that need to guide this work which have emerged through the experience of running these programmes are:

- There needs to be a particular focus on supporting the participation and leadership of women living in poverty or who suffer discrimination on the basis of aspects of their social identity such as disability, ethnicity, class, caste, HIV status, religion, or age.
- Work to support women's leadership will only advance poor women's interests if accompanied by long-term support for claiming and exercising their rights in other areas such as access to and control over resources, access to public services such as education and health, or protection from violence.
- Any support provided to prospective or elected women politicians must be carried out in as non-partisan a way as is possible.

A final important lesson concerns the need to base any programme work on an in-depth understanding of the particular gender issues facing a given community or organization, and hence the particular barriers to women's participation and leadership in that context. 'Gender audits' in the Philippines case study, the participatory needs assessment carried out by Oxfam GB's partner organization in Israel and the Occupied Palestinian Territories, and research undertaken by the civil-society 'observatories' in Chile all directly informed subsequent programme interventions and advocacy strategies that went on to have positive impacts for poor women.

Perhaps most significant to overcoming gender inequality, and the other forms of inequality and discrimination that keep women in poverty, is the work that feminist and women's rights organizations are already doing to articulate the needs of poor women, and to push for their strategic interests to be met. The work of just a few of these organizations – Movimiento de Mujeres por la Paz and Centro de Estudios de la Mujer in Honduras, Fanm Yo La in Haiti, Women for Prosperity in Cambodia, the 50/50 Group in Sierra Leone, and the Women's Budget Group in the UK – is profiled in these case studies. These groups, whether working at the local or national level, are made up of individuals who are already proving to be effective leaders, and are enabling other women to gain greater control over their lives, and to engage with their communities as active citizens.

About the author

Joanna Hoare and Fiona Gell wrote this chapter whilst working for Oxfam GB. Joanna now works as a freelance editor and writer on gender and development issues. Fiona is a gender and development specialist.

Notes

1. A.G. Jónasdóttir (1988) 'On the concept of interests, women's interests and the limitation of interest theory', in K.B. Jones and A.G. Jónasdóttir (eds.) *The Political Interests of Gender*, London: Sage Publications.

2. Women's Environment & Development Organization (WEDO), www.wedo.org (last accessed January 2008).
3. Women's Environment & Development Organization (WEDO) '50/50 Campaign Kit', www.wedo.org/campaigns.aspx?mode=5050campaignkit (last accessed January 2008).
4. M. Fleschman (2002) '"Gender budgets" seek more equity. Improved spending priorities can benefit all Africans', *Africa Recovery* 16:1, www.un.org/ecosocdev/geninfo/afrec/vol16no1/161wm.htm (last accessed January 2008).
5. For a review of the literature on the importance of a achieving a 'critical mass' of women in political institutions, see S. Grey (2001) 'Women and parliamentary politics. Does size matter? Critical mass and women MPs in the New Zealand House of Representatives', Paper for the 51st Political Studies Association Conference, 10–12 April 2001, Manchester, United Kingdom, www.capwip.org/readingroom/nz_wip.pdf (last accessed January 2008).
6. The Convention on the Elimination of All Forms of Discrimination against Women (CEDAW), adopted in 1979 by the UN General Assembly, is often described as an international bill of rights for women. Consisting of a preamble and 30 articles, it defines what constitutes discrimination against women and sets up an agenda for national action to end such discrimination (www.un.org/womenwatch/daw/cedaw/cedaw.htm – last accessed December 2007).
7. The Beijing Platform for Action, signed at the UN Fourth Conference on Women in Beijing in 1995, commits 189 signatory governments to 'take measures to ensure women's equal access to and full participation in decision-making and leadership…'. These measures include '[establishing] the goal of gender balance in governmental bodies and committees, as well as in public administrative entities, and in the judiciary, including … setting targets and implementing measures to substantially increase the number of women with a view to achieving equal representation of women and men, if necessary through positive action, in all governmental and public administration positions'. (www.wedo.org/campaigns.aspx?mode=5050 campaignkit – last accessed December 2007). This pledge was reiterated in 2006 at the 50th Commission on the Status of Women.
8. 'African Women Are Ready to Lead', *Africa Renewal*, July 2006, 7.
9. Women's Environment & Development Organisation (WEDO) 'The numbers speak for themselves', Fact Sheet no. 1, www.wedo.org/files/numbersspeak_factsh1.pdf (last accessed January 2008).
10. http://money.cnn.com/magazines/fortune/fortune500/2007/womenceos/ (last accessed January 2008).
11. United Nations (1995) *The World's Women 1995: Trends and Statistics,* New York: United Nations Statistics Division. Globally the gender gap in wages is hard to determine because so much data is not available. Within the industrial and services sector, the gap ranges between 53 per cent and 97 per cent with an average of 78 per cent (UNIFEM (2000) 'Biennial Report. Progress of the World's Women, 2000', New York: UNIFEM).
12. Inter-Parliamentary Union (www.ipu.org – last accessed December 2007).
13. WOMANKIND (www.womankind.org.uk/statistics.html – last accessed December 2007).

14. For instance, Rwanda's lower house has 48 per cent women, South Africa's Parliament 32.8 per cent, and Mozambique 34.8 per cent. Inter-Parliamentary Union (www.ipu.org/wmn-e/arc/classif300906.htm – last accessed December 2007).
15. S. Clisby (2005) 'Gender mainstreaming or just more male-streaming? Experiences of popular participation in Bolivia', *Gender and Development* 13(2): 23–35.
16. There are two types – reserved seats and legislative quotas. Most quotas prior to the 1990s were adopted voluntarily by political parties and, as such, were directed only at reserving seats in a single party via changes to selection practices. Over the last decade, however, a growing number of national legislatures have adopted legislative quotas – amending constitutions and electoral laws to mandate that all parties increase the percentage of women they nominate for local or national elections.
17. In Eritrea – a state with no democracy or accountability – the women elected via quotas have no power to influence government decisions and there is confusion among them about who they represent. In Tanzania, the use of reserved seats for women has taken the pressure off political parties to place women in the ballot and may have eroded the power of women to take their places in Parliament via the 'normal' routes (E. Ward (2006) 'Real or illusory progress? Electoral quotas and women's political participation in Tanzania, Eritrea and Uganda', *Trocaire Development Review*, 73–95, http://trocaire.org/pdfs/policy/developmentreview/2006/devrev2006.pdf – last accessed December 2007).

CHAPTER 2

Pa Kite M Deyo! Don't Leave Me Out! Haitian women demand their right to participate in public affairs

Kristie van Wetering

The legacy of years of violent political turmoil and entrenched ideas about gender roles makes it very difficult for women in Haiti to be active in the political arena, despite the fact that many have already proved themselves to be dynamic and able leaders of their communities. This chapter describes the work of women's rights organization Fanm Yo La *in mobilizing women to vote and to hold their elected representatives to account, and in supporting women candidates before and after elections.*

Introduction

Once known as the 'Pearl of the Antilles', Haiti is a country of paradoxes. It is rich in culture and beauty, yet economically extremely poor, and the ubiquitous Haitian spirit of hospitality is often overshadowed by widespread violence and insecurity. Despite an accent on community and co-operation, more than half of the population is marginalized and excluded: such is the plight of Haitian women.

In Haitian culture, women are highly regarded for their strength, persTeverance, and wisdom. At the same time, they are mother and wife, sister and daughter, teacher and family provider. They are referred to as the *'poto mitan'*[1] of Haitian society – the central beam, the foundation – keeping all things together. Numerous Haitian proverbs revere and respect women, professing that 'Se fanm ki ranje tab la, e se li ki ranje lavi a' (it is a woman who prepares the table, and it is she who prepares order in life).

It is surprising then, to witness the extent to which women are excluded from participating in so many aspects of Haitian life, and additionally the extent to which women are victims of violence and abuse.

A difficult life for Haitian women

The average Haitian woman is a master of multi-tasking, raising her children, keeping the home, and working long hours in difficult conditions to provide a meagre living. Often she does this alone, as at least 43 per cent of Haitian households are run by single mothers. Haitian girls were granted access to formal education in 1934, yet studies estimate that today only 17 per cent of girls finish secondary education.

Access to adequate health care for women remains a critical issue in a country that has the highest maternal mortality rate in the Western hemisphere (520 per 100,000 women) – a number that has actually increased over the last few years. Furthermore, it is estimated that eight out of ten women in Haiti are victims of domestic violence. It is also estimated that women contribute up to 70 per cent of the national economy through their participation in the informal sector, yet they enjoy less than 38 per cent of the profits generated by the economy.[2]

Women living in rural areas face particular difficulties. Eighty per cent of people living in rural communities in Haiti live in extreme poverty, and 'in a country so severely centralized, the rural poor are even more affected by blatant and systemic exclusion and marginalization – socially, economically, and politically. Again, women are doubly hit by this reality. Their voices are drowned out and silenced', affirms Yolette Etienne, Oxfam GB-Haiti Country Programme Manager.

Obstacles facing women in political life

Historically, women played a significant role in the slave revolution which brought about Haiti's independence from France in 1804, and several women stand out as key figures in Haiti's past. Haitians are even proud to boast that they had a female president for a brief time: as the first female Chief Justice of the Haitian Supreme Court from 1986–1990, Ertha Pascal-Trouillot became Haiti's first (and to date only) female president between two coup d'états in 1990.

However, for the most part, Haitian politics have always been *for* men and *by* men. The game of politics is organized according to men's rules, with male-designed structures and political tools. It was only in 1957 that women gained their full privileges to vote and to participate in the public arena. Since then, discriminatory legislation has continued to keep women at an unfair disadvantage against their male counterparts in all areas of life, as an inherent imbalance in power relations exists, from the basic traditional family unit, all the way up to institutional structures and decision-making arenas. This discrimination serves to exacerbate the effects of the poverty in which so many women in Haiti live, and their marginalization from political activity denies them the right to influence and input into policy decisions that could alleviate this poverty.

Furthermore, the women's movement in Haiti is sometimes seen in a less than positive light, due to negative perceptions and misconceptions that many people have regarding feminism, meaning that many men and women alike have been reluctant to associate themselves with it. Feminism is perceived by some Haitians as an attempt to replace men in their 'naturally' determined roles. In a country where many are conservative Christians, this is seen as non-Christian and therefore not acceptable.

Finally, Haiti's turbulent political history and past crises have done nothing to advance the position of Haitian women in everyday life, let alone politics. When a country is in crisis, the government is only concerned with the basic 'bread and butter' issues of politics: there is no room left to discuss other issues such as health care, education, and women's rights.

Democracy in the wake of tyranny and violence

When considering the question of women and politics in Haiti, it must be noted that the current difficulties that women face in entering politics are not just due to an unequal balance of power between men and women. The state of Haitian politics in general is also an important factor.

Following years of a brutal American occupation, more than 30 years of tyrant dictators, and several bloody coup d'états, the first free and democratic elections in Haiti were held in November 1990 with an impressively high voter turnout. Another violent coup followed nine months later, which was followed by three years of a vicious *de facto* government. With constitutional order restored in October 1994, the country experienced its first transfer of power from one democratically elected government to another in 1995. For five years the country enjoyed relative peace and stability. New elections were held in 2000, but accusations of fraud and corruption plunged the country into another violent political crisis that lasted for three years, culminating in the forced resignation of President Aristide in February 2004.

As Haiti continues to struggle along the path to democracy, a political culture where the rule of law is upheld and human rights are respected and promoted is slowly being developed. Yet many people still associate elections and politics with violence, hence affecting their notions of civic responsibility and their interest in participating in politics on any level. In addition, women have not been exempt from political violence, as candidates and non-candidates alike. During the Duvalier dictatorship (1957–1971), Lilianne Pierre-Paul, a journalist and political activist, started a call-in radio show where women were encouraged to voice their political and social opinions: as a result she was arrested and tortured. Upon release she left the country and spent several years in exile. Likewise, in 2003, two prominent female political activists, Carline Simon and Judie C. Roy (who eventually ran in the 2006 elections as a presidential candidate) were arrested and assaulted by Haitian police, allegedly operating on behalf of the ruling party.

Achievement in the face of resistance

Despite the challenges and obstacles, women have made some significant advances in the public arena over the past decade. Women's associations and groups have formed across the country, from the larger urban centres to small isolated communities in the country's most remote corners.

The creation of the Ministry of Women's Affairs and Women's Rights in 1994, charged with working to improve the conditions of Haitian women in all aspects of life, offers hope for a more systematic approach to responding to the needs and interests of women. One of the main objectives is to integrate women's issues into all aspects of public life: to place women's issues on the agendas of the Health, Education, and Justice Ministries, to name three key sectors where women's rights are systematically violated. While it took some time to develop strategies and find its unique voice, the Ministry of Women's Affairs and Women's Rights is making some significant advances. In addition, Haitian women have held various positions of authority within state organs, including that of Prime Minister, Director-General of the Haitian National Police, and the Chief General Inspector of the Haitian National Police.

Legislative changes made in 2005 mean that today, rape is considered a crime punishable by law, and numerous rape cases (including several against police officers) have gone to trial. Furthermore, the Haitian national police recently launched a campaign to recruit more women into the force.

Working to bring about change: Fanm Yo La takes action

Comprising more than half of the population of Haiti, there is no question that women are playing a crucial role in the country's development. Therefore, women must have *and enjoy* the right not only to participate, but also the right to be heard and listened to in matters of public policy and national development. Yet, due to the systematic and structural discrimination and exclusion of women in the affairs of public life and in decision-making arenas, women are at a great disadvantage when it comes to being successful candidates in national elections, or being chosen for positions of responsibility and authority.

This is precisely what the dedicated women of Fanm Yo La – the Haitian Women's Collective for the Participation of Women in Politics – are striving to change.

Since 1998, Fanm Yo La (which means 'Women are Here' in Haitian Creole) has been promoting women's civil and political rights in an effort to ensure that women play a more active role in policy and decision-making processes. Recognizing that systems and beliefs need to change, the organization is working towards the 'feminization' of political and public life via various activities focusing on two main areas. The first is generating awareness about women's issues and concerns within state structures, with the end goal of achieving a systematic integration of women's concerns and gender equality within public policy. The second is encouraging civil-society organizations, political parties, and women's organizations to be proactive in terms of promoting gender equity in their organizational structures, by providing and promoting access to positions of authority and responsibility to women from all socio-economic groups.

At the same time, Fanm Yo La's work is not just about encouraging women to take the challenge to run for president, or senator, or mayor. It is also about getting ordinary women – mothers and grandmothers, small-scale producers and peasant businesswomen – to realize that it matters what they think, that their votes count, and that they not only have the *right* but also the *responsibility* to make their voices heard. Thus, Fanm Yo La's work also includes motivating women to join together in solidarity and to participate actively in local and national politics by joining in the debates and going to the polls. In this way, Oxfam GB's support to organizations such as Fanm Yo La is crucial to empower Haitian women to make their voices heard.

'Once heard, Haitian women are then able to participate more fully in decisions that affect their lives as well as in the positive development of their communities. They are able to question, challenge, and even change their environments. Strong and active Haitian women means greater social, economic, and political wealth – which translates into healthier children with brighter futures.' (Yolette Etienne, Oxfam GB-Haiti Country Programme Manager)

Seeking out community leaders

'There are a lot of peasant women with experiences to share – experiences that can positively influence the future of our country.' (Lisa François, Executive Director of Fanm Yo La)

To disregard the experiences of peasant women does a blatant disservice to the country as it strives to pull itself out of its current state of poverty and underdevelopment. Fanm Yo La's efforts, therefore, seek to draw on the rich experiences of Haitian women from all walks of life and from all parts of the country. The women active in Fanm Yo La's activities share many similar characteristics. Ranging in age from 25 to 60, most of the women come from rural areas, where they are dynamic leaders in their communities. Most are active members of community-based organizations or associations, whether it be the local grain co-operative or the local church group, and most are women who already have some leverage within their communities. Some are small-scale businesswomen or market vendors, while others are teachers, church leaders, or voodoo priestesses.

While most have not finished high school and have limited reading and writing skills, these are the women who are in a position to influence the development of their communities through political involvement. As such, these are the women that Fanm Yo La seeks out – to build capacity, to strengthen and empower. These are the women at the heart of Fanm Yo La's activities and campaigns.

Elections 2006: mobilizing Haitian women and supporting female candidates

'This [citizen mobilization] initiative has been an excellent one. In general women are afraid to get involved, afraid to take responsibility and to participate [in politics]...but due to the civic education training combined with the awareness-generating and mobilization activities carried out, women have decided that they do not want to be left behind, they want to be out in front.' (Rosna Prévil, health educator, Grand Rivière du Nord)

In the two years leading up to the 2006 presidential, legislative, and municipal elections, Fanm Yo La, together with another local partner supported by Oxfam GB, carried out a national citizen-mobilization campaign in three northern and north-eastern municipalities. The overall aim of this campaign was to reinforce the democratic process and encourage the political participation of women at all levels, but particularly at the municipal level. At the same time Fanm Yo La used similar methods and techniques to carry out activities in other departments to ensure a broader national approach.

The campaign consisted of inter-connected activities. These included encouraging women to think more about their role in Haitian society and to find out about the various political platforms of different political parties and candidates, and getting women to commit to voting. Meetings and debates with local candidates, open to everyone in the community, provided spaces for dialogue. Workshops were also held on themes such as the importance of the elections for local authorities, the role of candidates and the different local authority positions, non-violent conflict resolution and management, and the role of women in public life.

With alarmingly high illiteracy rates, especially among women, radio is a crucial medium in Haiti. For this reason, Fanm Yo La and the other campaign organizers relied heavily on Haitian radio stations, more specifically community-based radio stations. Radio shows, commercials, and short broadcasts encouraging citizens to vote, and promoting the participation of Haitian women in the political process, were used to ensure the maximum target audience possible.

While the overall campaign targeted both men and women alike, Fanm Yo La placed a special emphasis on reinforcing the capacity of *female* candidates, political activists, and community leaders. Thematic training workshops designed to address the specific needs of these women were organized in the three target communities in the north and north-east as a way to provide additional support to the candidates. Themes included participative community management and local development, good governance, debate techniques, and campaign organization and techniques.

Lobbying activities aimed at the Provisional Electoral Council (CEP) resulted in the inclusion of an article in the electoral law stipulating that all political parties had to ensure that 30 per cent of their candidates are women. Additionally, together with female candidates from a number of municipalities,

Fanm Yo La prepared and submitted a list of demands to the CEP to request that action be taken to ensure the installation of voting offices in several communities which did not have them.

One of the creative initiatives of the project entailed the signing of protocol agreements with political candidates from all parties, both men and women alike. The protocols – based on the principles of decentralization, local power management, respect for human rights, and non-violence – seek to ensure greater accountability of local authorities with respect to community residents, to minimize exclusion, and promote co-operation and collaboration for the development of the community. Guided by the preamble of the Haitian Constitution of 1987 which calls for the government to ensure that the civil, political, social, economic, and cultural rights of all citizens are protected and promoted, the protocols were signed following community debates between candidates and local residents that sought to identify specific issues facing the communities relating to health, education, infrastructure, environment, and justice. Specific articles in the protocols included: mutual respect and courtesy during electoral campaigns; 'Town Hall' meetings to be held every three months to evaluate the council's activities during the previous months; publication of a regular news bulletin to keep the population informed on decisions made and actions taken; and the commitment to engage in promoting women's rights and the full participation of women via the integration of women into positions of responsibility and authority within the community.

The results: Haitian women make their voices heard

In the three municipalities where campaigning activities took place, the fruits of Fanm Yo La's efforts were visible. In Carice, the female candidate for the post of mayor was successfully elected, and in neighbouring Mont Organisé, six out of the seven female candidates were elected to their respective posts. In addition, women outnumbered men at the polls.

These results were echoed on a national level. A total of 4,000 female candidates ran in the elections; of these, 400 women were successfully elected to various posts. Most of the women were elected to local-government posts, with only eight women elected to Parliament – four as senators (out of a total of 30 seats), and four as deputies (out of a total of 98 seats). Even though the number of women in Parliament is far from high enough, the overall numbers speak volumes when compared to the numbers recorded for the elections of 2000; in those elections, of 2,037 women candidates, 161 were elected.

Responding to the challenges and responsibilities of being an elected leader

'We have won the first step! Now we need to persevere to the second!' declared Fanm Yo La's director Lisa François at a public ceremony to celebrate those women who ran in the elections, as well as a number of key women involved in the mobilization campaign. To the words of the song '*Pa Kite m Deyo*' (Don't Leave Me Out), plaques of achievement and encouragement were presented by current and former female politicians.

Recognizing that getting women into positions of power and decision-making is only the first step, Fanm Yo La's approach entails providing continued support to newly elected officials. 'It is about transforming the candidates into leaders, into positive role models for change', says François when asked about what comes next. 'It is about assisting female officials to achieve their mission related to their respective posts, whether it be in the Parliament or in their local communities as mayors and/or community representatives', she adds.

Once elected, women leaders face a series of challenges and obstacles to overcome. Perhaps the most obstructive is the mind-set of their male counterparts, many of whom still struggle with sexist attitudes towards women. Another challenge is trying to involve more women in the community in confronting questions related to community management and development. To address this issue, Fanm Yo La is working with 120 of the 400 elected female leaders at the local level. Joint workshops are being held with local governments in a selection of municipalities in five departments, specifically targeting mayors and their deputies, men and women alike. The three-day workshops seek to combine training on community management with training on gender equity, via presentations on participative community management and local development, and good governance.

Fanm Yo La is optimistic about the workshops. 'In the areas where we are working, the cartels of many of the mayors elected include at least one woman. If we can facilitate the enlightenment of the male mayors [regarding] specific women's issues, than we have two out of three on a team working to seek greater gender equity and integration', says François.

Additionally, women leaders, particularly at the level of the senate and chamber of deputies, may require additional support to increase their capacity and effectiveness relating to specific issues and/or technical skills. One such example is that of judicial and legislative reform, specifically in terms of ensuring gender equity in the revision of laws. For the eight female parliamentarians currently in office, Fanm Yo La recently organized a two-day workshop with a prominent human-rights lawyer and former senator and deputy. During these workshops, an inventory of discriminatory legislation was prepared and analysed via a series of tools and exercises. Additionally, the women were trained on preparing proposed bills for new and reformed legislation.

Looking forward to elections in 2010

Piti piti zwazo a ap fè niche li.
Little by little the bird builds its nest.

This popular Haitian proverb aptly describes Fanm Yo La's sentiments following the last round of elections. Slowly but surely women are gaining the confidence of their fellow citizens and being chosen to hold positions of power and decision-making. They are carving out a place for their positions, ideas, perspectives, and recommendations, proving that Haitian women have a crucial role to play in determining the future of the country.

But there is still much to be done.

With a lack of credible and sufficiently professional political parties in the field, the work is not easy. Fanm Yo La will continue to lobby for the respect of the '30 per cent rule' in terms of female candidates. Lobbying the government to encourage respect for gender equity and to promote the full participation of women when appointing cabinet ministers will also be a continuing activity, as at present, only two cabinet ministers in the current government are women.

Likewise, Fanm Yo La will continue to prepare today's women to be tomorrow's leaders. With the support of Oxfam GB, the organization's 'Women in Politics School' will provide training for approximately 50 women from the western department. The classes, which will be held on a weekly basis, will cover many of the topics covered in training sessions run during the campaign.

As more and more women are elected to official posts, demonstrating their capacity and ability to play crucial roles within the national public arenas, they will serve as role models and agents of change, positively influencing the culture of politics for the next generation of women. And as Haitian women in both rural and urban settings become increasingly active as fully fledged citizens with a voice and the right to be heard, Haiti is slowly moving towards the day when women all over the country enjoy a life in which they are treated with equality and respect.

About the author

Kristie van Wetering wrote this chapter while she was Media and Communications Officer for Oxfam GB in Haiti.

Notes

1. The *poto mitan* is the central post in a voodoo temple that serves as the connection between the spiritual and physical world; it is the conduit for the spirits to enter the physical world during a voodoo ceremony.
2. *Foire d'Opinions Haitiennes (2007), excerpt from* 'Status of Women', Marie Carmel Paul-Austin, Published by TiCam, www.haitiwebs.com/forums/relationships/43018-status-women-haiti.html (last checked 17 August 2007).

CHAPTER 3

Creating the space to empower women fishers: lessons from the Philippines

Aurora Urgel and Gaynor Tanyang

Oxfam GB's Leadership Development Programme for Women works with four partners in the Philippines. The work involves assessing how far gender is mainstreamed into programme work, and developing action plans to ensure that women working in the fishing industry play a more active role in community-based coastal resource management and in designing fisheries policy reforms. In the course of this work, participants identified the steps necessary to establish a favourable environment for encouraging and supporting more women to become leaders in the fishing sector.

Introduction

Poverty in the Philippines

The Philippines is an archipelago of 7,100 islands off the coast of South-East Asia, with a population of 88 million people. While overall poverty rates have fallen continuously since the early 1980s, very high rates of population growth and the unequal distribution of income mean that over a third of the population live in poor households. Rates of poverty in rural and coastal areas remain particularly high. Wealth and the control of resources remains concentrated in the hands of a few. Natural disasters and conflict are almost constant threats to people's lives and livelihoods, particularly in coastal areas. About 19–20 typhoons hit the country annually, and the series of fault zones that crisscross the archipelago produces an average of five earthquakes per day.

Fishing is one of the country's most important industries, and yet despite this, those working as fishers themselves, or working in fish processing, are amongst the poorest and most marginalized people in Philippine society. Not only are their livelihoods precarious due to the ever-present threat of natural disasters, but they have also been adversely affected by the impacts of trade liberalization, and have had little opportunity to influence the policies of the Philippine government in this regard. In this context, women working in the fishing industry are doubly marginalized, both by their dependence on such a precarious and exploited means of livelihood, and by their lack of visibility as major economic contributors within the industry.

Women in the fishing industry

Women's contributions to the fishing industry in the Philippines are diverse, but often undervalued and unrecognized. While fishing itself is mainly done by men, some women do fish, and others are engaged in a host of directly linked activities, such as mending nets, boat maintenance, fish-/shrimp-fry collection,[1] and fish farming, as well as processing, packing, and marketing fish once it has been caught. These activities are vital for the survival and operation of the fishing industry, but as they are considered to be extensions of women's social functions or domestic responsibilities rather than income-generating work, they are seldom given economic value, and are frequently overlooked in assessments of the fishing industry and those working in it. This is despite the fact that the income from women's activities makes an important contribution to the well-being of households dependent on fishing. Most of these households are poor, and affected as a result by poor health, poor nutrition, low rates of educational enrolment and attainment, limited income, and low community participation.[2] As such, any efforts to improve the visibility, working conditions, control over resources, and incomes of women fishers are likely to have direct, positive repercussions for poverty alleviation within these communities.

But barriers to women's full participation in coastal resource management persist, not least in women's own acceptance of the gender division of labour prevailing in most coastal communities. Most women believe that men are the head of the family, and should support the family financially, and handle a heavy workload. Women, meanwhile, should attend to all the problems and needs of the family and household. This partly explains why in grassroots organizations in coastal communities, women fishers are largely active working on issues related to their reproductive roles in society. Leadership and decision-making positions on economic issues are dominated by men; when women do take on leadership roles, it is often in less influential positions such as secretary or treasurer – positions traditionally assigned to women because of the view that they pay more attention to detail and are better at budgeting.

That said, things are beginning to change. Effective and sustainable community-based management of coastal resources is acknowledged as an important means of helping to lift fishing communities out of poverty. Within community-based coastal resource management (CBCRM) projects, advocated by Oxfam GB and other non-state actors, women are now recognized as major stakeholders in this management process. As a result, fisherfolk organizations have put in place mechanisms for greater visibility and participation of women in leadership structures. But so far, these initiatives have failed to recognize that women's capacity to assume leadership positions is affected by limits on their mobility, the multiple burden of productive and reproductive work, and gender stereotyping. Women have little time or opportunity to take on management tasks, receive training and information, or establish contacts. There is little support in fisherfolk organizations for raising awareness of women's opinions and needs in this regard. This is because of the imbalance between women and men in leadership structures, and because of limited opportunities for training, and inappropriate approaches to capacity-building for women.

The Leadership Development Programme for Women

Working with four Oxfam GB partner organizations between March 2005 and December 2007, the Leadership Development Programme for Women (LDPW) was an initiative to identify women leaders in the fishing industry and support them to advocate their specific interests in the overall practice of coastal resource management. The key objectives of the project are:

- to enable women fishers to become effective and influential leaders within the four partner organizations, in recognition of the fact that women fishers have important skills and experience to bring to such positions, and that having more women in leadership positions will lead to better working conditions and economic outcomes for women fishers;
- to improve gender mainstreaming within these organizations, through assessing the extent to which current organizational structures and processes are responsive to gender issues and concerns;
- to design and support action plans addressing women's needs and interests;
- to encourage men and women within the fishing industry to take responsibility for supporting policies to increase the number of women in positions of leadership; and
- to contribute to greater learning on gender mainstreaming in CBCRM programmes, advocacy, and campaigns.

The LDPW Project consists of four stages: *assessing where we are* (gender audit); *defining our paths to empowerment* (planning); *walking together along the paths to empowerment* (implementation); and *learning and sharing creatively* (assessment process).

Stage 1: Assessing where we are (gender audit)

To begin with, the project analysed the extent to which each partner organization had succeeded in addressing gender issues in their policies and programmes. This included an assessment of training needs and gaps regarding gender mainstreaming, using participatory rapid appraisal methods to produce information on gender awareness and organizational structure. The results formed the basis for the next stage in the project, i.e. planning activities that would strengthen women's capacities and opportunities for participation and leadership within each organization.

Stage 2: Defining our paths to empowerment (planning)

At this stage, during four-day gender planning workshops, partner organizations were encouraged to identify gender issues of particular relevance to their area of work, and having done this, to formulate gendered action plans. Workshops also included leadership training. The action plans included developing a better knowledge about laws relating to women's rights and to the fishing industry.

Stage 3: Walking together along the paths to empowerment (implementation)

In this phase of the project, each partner organization undertook its own, targeted activities, based on the information that they had collected in stage one, and the plans they had drawn up in stage two of the project. The partners' experiences in implementing these activities now follow.

Assessing the gender impact of trade liberalization in fisheries

The Fisherfolk Movement (Kilusang Mangingisda or KM) coalition was formed in 2001 to unite marginalized fisherfolk in addressing the threats of the Philippine government's policy of trade liberalization in fisheries, introduced in the early 1990s. The women's committee, the Kababaihan ng Kilusang Mangingisda (KKM), was formed two years later by women representing different fishing organizations, in recognition of the need to mainstream women's concerns into the anti-trade liberalization agenda.

As part of LDPW, KKM conducted research on the impact of trade liberalization in fisheries on milkfish fry-gathering. The study revealed that privatizing fry hatcheries, which is in line with the government's liberalization strategy to boost agricultural production, has had a damaging impact on women's livelihoods. Women gatherers of milkfish fry have been displaced from their source of income because fry buyers shifted their demand to private hatchery suppliers. As women's income from fry-gathering is used to finance the education of their children, this in turn is affecting their children's futures. These findings will be used to inform KM's campaign against ongoing trade liberalization, as well as providing leverage for the women's committee to press for greater involvement of women in decision-making processes within the organization, on the basis that addressing issues particularly affecting women has benefits for the whole community. For while the women's committee holds one seat on the KM Executive Committee, until 2004 this seat did not have voting privileges, and the Committee remains male-dominated. KM also needs to do much more to nurture women's leadership skills and competencies, and to review its organizational policies to ensure that barriers to women's full representation are addressed.

Advancing women's rights in fisheries management and articulating the voice of women fishers in policy reforms

'Budyong' means conch shell, used in many coastal communities as a horn to make announcements or attract attention. When deciding on a name for their new network, women fishers chose the name Budyong as a symbol of women's voices, and of the need for them to be heard in the fishing industry.

Budyong began life in 2003 as an informal task force to contribute to the gender analysis of the Fisheries Code, introduced in 1998 after ten years of lobbying. Prior to this, women fishers' participation in public debate and lobbying on the Fisheries Code had been minimal. Obstacles to participation included the need to obtain their husband's permission to join activist organizations and to leave the house to take part in activities, as well as a lack of time, as a result of their unending work in the home, caring for children and aged or sick parents. As a result, almost all fisherfolk organizations, from the barangay[3] to municipal and national levels were led by men, so that women were not well-represented in national consultations on fisheries policy reforms. In addition, development programme work within the fishing sector always targeted men. Generally, women were not considered as a distinct group of workers in the sector, and their interests were subsumed in the dominant development agenda. This was despite the fact that women participated in resource management in their own communities, undertaking vital tasks such as cooking, cleaning, budgeting, and logistics.

The realization that they as women fishers shared the same experiences of being marginalized was a wake-up call to action for the members of Budyong. Thus, from an informal structure, the women resolved to strengthen their ranks and establish themselves as a network to represent the interests of women fishers from the local to the national level. LDPW paved the way for the formal establishment of the network, which consists of local women's organizations from different fishing municipalities in the Philippines.

Based on the experiences and demands of their members, Budyong has developed an advocacy agenda consisting of:

- recognition of women's priority use rights in fisheries;
- recognition of women as stakeholders in fisheries development;
- security of housing and land tenure for fishing households;
- delivery of comprehensive health care services; and
- advocacy for women's representation in the Local Sectoral Representation (LSR) bill.

Budyong was successful in influencing the Comprehensive National Fisheries Industry Plan, which is the government's draft 20-year plan for the sector, to include provisions to address women fishers' issues. These included carrying out a gender analysis of the current situation in the fishing sector, assessing in particular the as yet unrecognized contribution of women in the domestic fisheries industry. Other provisions related to using gender indicators in data collection, developing and implementing a policy of gender mainstreaming, institutionalizing women fishers' participation in policy making bodies, and putting consultative mechanisms in place. In addition, in a dialogue with the National Fisheries and Aquatic Resource Management Council (NFARMC), Budyong with other women fishers and gender advocates were able to get commitment from NFARMC to ensure that women fishers would be invited to participate during NFRAMC meetings, albeit as observers (i.e. without voting power).

Responding to violence against women in the community

On the island of Tabon, Aklan province, Oxfam GB partner Developers provided support to four fisherfolk associations through the LDPW to address violence against women (VAW) in their communities, and to raise awareness of the national 'Anti-Violence Against Women and their Children' (Anti-VAWC) law, passed in 2004.

As part of the gender-audit process carried out at the start of the project, Developers asked men and women in Tabon whether they knew of any cases of VAW. They unanimously responded that VAW was not happening in their community. Subsequently, during training carried out with women from the community, participants were asked to draw their 'river of life', representing all the things that had happened to them since they were born. One by one, women told stories of how they were beaten by their fathers as young children, or saw their mothers being beaten, or that their husbands beat them when drunk. One woman who had left her husband shared how she was made to feel ashamed by other members of the community, because she was now a single mother.

The participants learned that men – their own husbands and fathers – do not have the right to inflict violence on women and their children, and that the law states that violence within a marital relationship should not be dismissed as merely a 'private issue'. Furthermore, they learned that the government and the community have an obligation to protect women and children from any abuse.

The women set out to take what they had learned about the Anti-VAWC law into their community, conducting training on VAW themselves. They persuaded a man who had, in the past, been violent towards his children, to take part in a role play depicting how he had behaved. The father accepted this challenge because after realizing years before that what he was doing was not right, he wanted to let other fathers know that they too could change. This alone made a positive impact by raising awareness within the community on VAWC.

Through participating in this training and developing their own skills as leaders and educators, the women have come to realize that there is a clear link between VAW and the general tendency for men to limit women's opportunities to participate in formal organizations outside the home, impacting on their capacity to assume leadership positions. In light of this, along with

Developers, the women of Tabon have been steadfast in influencing local development plans to address gender-based violence as a matter of local policy.

Mainstreaming gender in an organizational context

SAMMACA is a fisherfolk organization, established in 1992 to promote the community's right to manage their coastal resources. The results of the organization's gender audit showed that while women were fairly well-represented in positions of leadership, and while the organization had worked on gender issues since the mid 1990s, the concerns of women working in the industry were not being adequately addressed, and leadership remained very male-orientated. This meant that the development agenda focused on male fishers' concerns, and those considered to be 'major community issues' such as illegal fishing and privatization of coastal areas, while gender issues, such as women's multiple burden of productive and reproductive work, and violence within the family, remained marginalized. Prior to 2004, women's concerns were not something the male leaders felt they needed to address and act on.

The plan that was developed from this analysis focused on transforming women's and men's attitudes to gender inequality. As part of this, Oxfam GB worked with SAMMACA to make its standard training on leadership more gender-responsive.

One unintended but very positive result of the LDPW was the development of a young generation of gender facilitators and advocates (aged 22–32), who at the time of the project's implementation formed the core of SAMMACA's community organizers. Two young women still serve in the organization; one was recently elected as general secretary. The recommendations of the gender audit were also considered during the organization's recent strategic-planning process. As a result, the identification of resources to be managed by women, the development of a gender-responsive education curriculum, and advocacy for the establishment of community-based responses to VAWC have all been included in the strategic plan, paving the way for more women to participate in resource management and to realize their potential as leaders.

Step 4: Learning and sharing creatively (assessment process)

One tool used to assess the project has been a theatre presentation depicting the reflections and experiences of women participants. This provided a conducive learning atmosphere where women were able to express their views on leadership development and their empowerment in a creative way. The songs and poems developed by the women are now being used in trainings as an aid to the learning process.

Lessons learned about developing women's leadership

Developing gender-responsive leadership training

The LDPW included a specific course of leadership training for women from the four partner organizations. During this, participants discussed whether women and men exercise leadership differently. The women's views reflected the realities about how women and men are perceived as leaders. Women are seen as 'soft', emotional, and unable to make up their mind (character traits that are considered to make them less effective as leaders), while men are seen as strong, rational, and reliable. On the other hand, women are thought to consider the different aspects of an issue when making a decision more carefully than men, who can be unyielding when they make decisions. These assumptions illustrate the gender biases prevalent in these communities, as the participants came to realize. In addition, the participants recognized that existing opportunities for leadership within their organizations were not the same for the two sexes, with women being confined to less influential roles as secretaries and treasurers, despite their potential capacity to contribute more.

Existing leadership-training modules rarely take gender into consideration as a factor in leadership development, despite it having considerable influence, as the insights from the participants in the LDPW training show. This is why the objective of the training for women leaders was not only to develop women's capacities to lead within their organizations and communities, but also to transform the strategies of leadership development itself, based on the following principles:

- Leadership is exercised not only in positions of authority. Leadership is exercised when parents teach their children the positive values of love, respect, citizenship, and service. Leadership is manifested when people help each other to achieve a common goal, such as reporting illegal fishing activities.
- Women and men are leaders with equal potential to contribute to change in society. But women, as a result of their historical oppression, do not have equal access to positions of power, influence, and decision-making.
- Leadership is a process of dialogue that should be inclusive of and sensitive to the varying levels of marginalization and inequality in societies, resulting from differences in sex, class, age, ethnicity, and other factors.[4]
- Leadership training should be empowering. It is based on the recognition of the dignity of every individual, and the fact that in each person, woman or man, rich or poor, educated or less educated, lies the potential to be an effective leader.
- Leadership that is empowering embodies the value of participatory governance; decisions are made not by individuals working alone, but by people working together to find solutions to their problems. However,

participation can only be meaningful and effective if it is inclusive of everyone, most importantly the marginalized and oppressed.

Creating a women-friendly environment for leadership development

In the fisherfolk movement, most grassroots organizations have more female than male members, but men dominate in leadership positions. Why are women afraid to take on the challenge and responsibility of a leadership position even when it is 'offered' to them? The answers are simple: women do not want to add to their already heavy burden of managing the household and working outside the home; they fear they will have to stretch not only their meagre budget but also their limited time even further; and many are afraid of speaking in a crowd. Therefore, creating an environment favourable for women to develop their leadership skills requires that these factors are taken into account and addressed in the policies of the organization and their ways of working.

Going through the gender audit enabled the partner organizations to reflect on what stage they had reached in terms of gender mainstreaming, and to identify and analyse the barriers to women's participation in their organization's activities and leadership structure. The process highlighted the importance of collecting data on the numbers of women who participate in activities, and what kind of tasks they undertake, and of examining the extent to which fisherfolk organizations, through their CBCRM programmes, address specific gender issues, including women's leadership development.

As a result of the gender audit, the organizations involved in this project were able to identify the following as necessary for creating an environment for women's leadership to grow:

- reviewing organizational policies to measure how they explicitly or implicitly marginalize women's concerns;
- integrating a gender perspective into the planning cycle by incorporating specific goals, objectives, indicators, and activities;
- raising men's awareness and support to achieve gender equality;
- sharing the responsibility of gender mainstreaming within the entire leadership structure, and not just with women's committees or gender focal persons;
- providing opportunities for alternative forms of articulation and expression, including the use of visual and performance arts, in programme activities;
- recognizing differences *between* women, for instance understanding that older and younger women have different skills and experience to bring to leadership and decision-making, and facilitating the exchange of knowledge and ideas between women of different ages; and
- linking with other women's organizations in the Philippines (this enabled women fishers' concerns to be integrated into the advocacy agenda of the

mainstream women's movement, giving recognition to the specific issues of women fishers as separate but related to issues faced by other women in Philippine society, particularly rural women).

Practical consideration in terms of the physical environment, locality, and timing should also be conducive to learning. This can be achieved by:

- providing a dedicated physical space for women to learn in, as well as to reflect, share their experiences with other women, find relief from their tensions and frustrations, and think about their own well-being and interests;
- ensuring that the training schedule is not in conflict with children's school activities or other community activities where women participate;
- providing child-care services at the training venue;
- scheduling activities in advance so that women can organize their household responsibilities around them; and
- providing a mix of training venues within the community and outside. Activities outside the community can provide relief for women, and allow them to explore places they normally would not be able to visit, but providing activities organized within the community helps to prevent household conflicts by ensuring that women participating in leadership training activities do not have to be away from home very often.

Encouraging women leaders to be advocates for gender equality

The prevailing notion is that traditionally, women who have succeeded in becoming leaders are those who have demonstrated effective communication skills, assertiveness, and the ability to function within the existing status quo. But these 'strong women' do not necessarily adopt an agenda that is favourable to women and other disempowered groups. Therefore, LDPW recognized that it is important to develop women not only as leaders but also as advocates for women's empowerment and gender equality, by encouraging participants to be more gender-aware, and to conduct their own gender analysis. Of course, running gender-sensitivity workshops alone does not equip women with the skills to implement their development agenda. Thus, there is a need gradually to improve women's competencies to translate gender analysis into achievable interventions, such as, in this case, CBCRM research, training, fisheries management, policy advocacy, and livelihoods development.

Moving forward: recommendations for programme development

The outcomes of the LDPW can be summed up as gaining recognition of two things: the validity and urgency of recognizing women's contributions to the fishing sector and its development, and the need to identify and support women leaders within the industry who are able to articulate women's interests, and ensure that they are on the agenda of organizations working in this sector.

On an individual level, these interventions helped women to build their self-confidence, appreciate their own abilities, and realize that they had the potential to assume leadership positions.

From the outset, LDPW recognized that strategies promoting gender equality are central to addressing the pressing challenges women face in attaining positions of economic leadership. Some of the strategies successfully implemented in this project include:

- ensuring women's participation in the entire programme cycle: problem analysis; planning; implementation; evaluation;
- making available resources, particularly human and financial resources, to address gender issues and to encourage more women and men to become advocates for gender equality;
- setting up mechanisms at the organizational and programme level for men and women to discuss, negotiate, and agree on priority gender issues and interventions;
- working with men to increase their awareness of the relevance of gender issues, and to encourage their support for women leaders and gender-mainstreaming initiatives;
- providing spaces for women-only initiatives to enable them to act autonomously in project management, decision-making, and fund management.

Overall, these projects demonstrate that leadership training which addresses gender issues can play a vital role in correcting the imbalances that exist in prevailing economic power structures in society, in this case by highlighting the crucial role that women play in the Philippines fishing industry and in coastal management, and empowering them to participate fully in decision-making. In order to counter these imbalances, and in addition to changing institutional structures and policies, both women and men need to be empowered with the appropriate skills, knowledge, resources, and motivation. If we are to achieve real social transformation, we need to recognize that, given equal opportunities, we all have the power within us to become leaders ourselves.

About the author

Aurora Urgel wrote this chapter while working for Oxfam GB as a Programme Officer for the LDPW Project. Gaynor Tanyang was the consultant for the project. Aurora is now a consultant for the Asian Development Bank and Gaynor is working with a national rural women's network (Pambansang Koalisyon ng Kababaihan sa Kanayunan).

Notes

1. A fish 'fry' is a recently hatched fish that can already hunt its own food (http://en.wikipedia.org/wiki/Spawn_%28biology%29#Fry last accessed September 2007).
2. Data gathered from the 12 priority bays under the fisheries sector programme in the early 1990s show that at that time, the average annual income of fishing households was P25,426 ($509), way below the poverty threshold (Government of the Philippines n.d., draft 'Comprehensive National Fisheries Industry Development Plan', Manila: Government of the Philippines).
3. The *barangay* is the smallest political unit in the Philippines, consisting of a community of 2,000–5,000 people. It is often referred to as a local village.
4. M. Afkhami, A. Eisenberg, and H. Vaziri (2001) *Leading to Choices: A Leadership Training Handbook for Women,* Bethesda, Maryland: Women's Learning Partnership for Rights, Development, and Peace, www.learningpartnership.org/docs/engltcmanual.pdf (last accessed November 2007).

CHAPTER 4

Strengthening the voices of women leaders: lessons from Cambodia

Menh Navy

Contributor: Tath Bunheng

Recent reforms mean women in Cambodia now have the opportunity to stand for election to local councils. But many women councillors face discrimination and hostility from their male colleagues, and feel that they lack the skills and confidence to carry out their roles effectively. This chapter describes the work of Women For Prosperity, which has helped many women councillors in Cambodia to challenge discrimination, forge positive working relationships with their colleagues, and fulfil their responsibilities as elected officials to the people in their communities.

Introduction

Despite recent improvements in economic growth, and a reduction in the numbers of people living in absolute poverty, Cambodia remains one of the poorest countries in South-East Asia. In rural areas, poverty is particularly extreme, a problem compounded by the fact that thus far, the Cambodian government has failed to extend the social services such as health care and sanitation that could reduce people's vulnerability to the effects of poverty. Women, children, disabled people, elderly people, and ethnic minority groups are particularly affected by poverty in rural areas. Women, for example, have significantly lower educational attainment levels, literacy rates, and access to public services than men. Central government has traditionally been characterized by a lack of transparency, limited mechanisms of accountability, and corruption, leaving poor people with little opportunity to contribute to decision-making, which is heavily concentrated in some key ministry offices, such as the Prime Minister's office, the Ministry of Economy and Finance, and the Ministry of the Interior. Culture reinforces the authoritarian style of governance, since many Cambodians relegate decision-making authority to elites who have power in their communities. Poor, rural women in particular lack opportunities to participate in decision-making. Although the government has indicated a commitment to increase the number of women in decision-making positions, little progress has been made and targets are unlikely to be met.

At the local level, poor women and men's lack of voice means that local development plans have traditionally not reflected their priorities. In recognition of this, in 2001, the royal government of Cambodia introduced a policy of decentralization, with the aim of strengthening pluralist local democracy, promoting local and economic development, and reducing poverty. Following the introduction of the decentralization policy, local-level commune (or *sangkat*) elections were held in Cambodia for the first time in 2002.[1]

Women For Prosperity

It is in this social and political context that Oxfam GB's partner Women For Prosperity (WFP) works. WFP was formed on 1 July 1994 as an independent, non-profit, non-government organization. Its aims are to enable women to support their families economically and to experience personal safety and security, while maintaining their values and identity. WFP also seeks to empower women in the recognition and exercise of their rights, on equal terms with men, through leadership training, advocacy, lobbying, media campaigns, and awareness-raising with government officials, policy makers, and the general public. Activities have included training courses on 'Women's Legal Rights and Advocacy' and 'Human Rights, Women's Rights and Democracy'. These have been offered to female and male local-government and NGO officials, and are designed to equip participants with the tools necessary to become human-rights and women's-rights activists so they can in turn influence decision-makers at all levels.

WFP recognized that the introduction of decentralization and the announcement of local, commune-level elections provided an important opportunity for women in rural areas to enter local government and to participate in decision-making that would impact directly on the welfare of their communities. As such, WFP developed a comprehensive training programme for women who wished to stand for election in 2002, which was offered to 5,527 female candidates from all political parties. In the event, relatively few women were actually elected (only 977 [8.7 per cent] of the 11,261 councillors elected were women). But significantly, 34 women were elected as commune chiefs; prior to this, no woman had ever occupied this position.

Many of the women who were elected in 2002 found carrying out their duties as councillors very difficult. In response to this, since 2004 WFP has provided ongoing support and training to all female commune councillors, in partnership with Oxfam GB and other donors. This has taken the form of training on 'Women and Good Governance', as well as the establishment of a national women's network and a series of national-level Female Councillor Forums (FCFs). These forums allow women councillors from all political backgrounds to share experiences and learning, build solidarity, and advocate and lobby policy makers on gender and development issues. Participating in these activities has strengthened the confidence and skills of women councillors, enabling them to fulfil their professional duties to a higher standard, and to realize their potential as leaders of their communities. The women councillors' network has now been recognized by the Ministry of the Interior, which may in future provide funding towards it.

Barriers to women's active participation in local government

The low numbers of women elected in 2002 reflect the considerable obstacles that women face to participating in local government and other decision-making institutions in Cambodia. Low levels of education among women mean that many feel they do not have the skills, experience, or qualifications to act as representatives of their community. In addition, high levels of poverty force many women to focus on earning money to support their families, which means that they do not have sufficient funds to stand for election. Some women also feel politics is simply men's work in which women should not be involved. Perceptions that women are not capable of serving as councillors and that women's participation in government is 'inappropriate' also discourage women from standing for election. The patronage system and the active role of traditional authorities in Cambodia's patriarchal society undermine the creation of democratic, inclusive local governance by making it very difficult for anyone who does not already enjoy a high status in the community to get elected. This particularly affects women, who are less likely than men to have the right connections, or the wealth, to benefit from the patronage system. It also means that if they are elected, women councillors may be under pressure to serve the interests of powerful members of their community, rather than those who are poorer and more marginalized; this diminishes their ability to be accountable to local women.

The small number of women representatives in local government is in itself a significant issue, but just as important in the context of promoting women's leadership is the fact that many of the women who were elected did not feel able to perform their new roles to a high standard. Immediately after the 2002 elections, many women councillors reported that their capacity to take up their new responsibilities as councillors was limited. They felt unable to assert themselves during council meetings, and they knew that this would impact on their ability to raise issues of concern to them, relating to marginalized groups and poor people (particularly women and children). They were also worried about how they would balance their council duties with their traditional household, family, and child-care responsibilities. Some female councillors also reported being marginalized by their male counterparts.

Removing barriers and empowering women councillors: Female Councillor Forums (FCFs)

WFP recognized the importance of empowering and supporting the women councillors who were elected in 2002, in order that they would be able to serve as effective leaders in their communes. So in 2004 the organization shifted its programme focus from capacity-building on women's legal rights to developing a network for women commune councillors from across the political spectrum, and providing training at a series of Female Councillor Forums (FCFs).

The FCFs aim to improve the work performance of participants and to address the special challenges facing many female councillors: low confidence; lack of experience in office; discrimination from male colleagues; lack of family support; and low visibility as elected officials. The forums are open to all women councillors, rather than being targeted at those from particularly poor or marginalized backgrounds, because these are issues that affect women councillors regardless of their political or social background, given the highly patriarchal hierarchical nature of Cambodian society. And in fact, the majority of women elected in the 2002 commune elections came from poor households anyway.

In 2005 FCFs were run in seven pilot provinces (Battambang, Pursat, Svay Rieng, Siem Reap, Kampong Cham, Kampong Thom, and Kandal), with financial and technical support from Oxfam GB and other donors. Participants came from different communes and districts in each province, and represented different political parties. Following the success of the FCFs run in 2005, forums have since been run each year in nine provinces.

Learning from each others' experience

At each forum, the women councillors who are participating are asked by the WFP facilitator to decide the objectives for the forum. Common objectives identified at each forum have so far included:

- Strengthen self-confidence and leadership skills
- Build skills to improve female councillor performance
- Strengthen co-operation and solidarity among female councillors
- Form a network to share experience and provide mutual support
- Jointly develop strategies to solve the problems participants face in their work
- Make women councillors more visible in council affairs
- Develop participants' public presentation skills

Participants are also asked to identify particular issues and problems that they would like to discuss. At the forums, participants have identified a wide range of issues that they feel are impacting on their capacity to fulfil their roles effectively. These include lack of personal finances; the challenges of balancing their household responsibilities and their work as councillors; lack of support from their husbands; a low standard of living; and domestic violence. Once participants have come up with a list of issues, the facilitator then asks the women councillors to prioritize one or two issues that they wish to address at the forum, before dividing them into small groups to discuss how they would approach this problem. Within their groups, those with experience of dealing with this particular issue successfully are asked to explain what they did, and how it worked; those who have made unsuccessful attempts to deal with this issue are also asked to share their experiences. In this way, participants are able to learn from each others' experiences, and to work together to develop a strategy to address the particular issue in question, which can then be implemented by each councillor once she returns to her commune. The important thing in this exercise is that every participant must have the opportunity to contribute, as agreed in the ground rules for the exercise. In this way, this exercise promotes the self-confidence of each individual, and emphasizes that each individual idea is valuable and important.

Box 4.1 Challenging discrimination against women councillors

One issue identified at many of the FCFs was the overt discrimination faced by many women councillors. Working together in small groups, participants at the FCF were asked to define the issue and its cause, as they saw it, and to come up with a list of actions that each councillor could implement back in her commune. Below is an example of the outcomes of one such discussion.

Issue identified:
Discrimination against female councillors; male councillors failing to value the work of female councillors

Suggested cause:
Divisions within the commune council, and party politics

Some strategies for action:
- Each political party to call a meeting of their own members to discuss the problem
- Set up and respect ground rules to give each council member an opportunity to speak at meetings, and for other council members to listen respectfully without interrupting
- Encourage discussion about women and men sharing responsibilities
- Set up a reporting and evaluation system, involving all members
- Encourage each member to understand their role and responsibilities, as well as those of the commune council as a whole
- Give women councillors the opportunity to attend training (e.g. district training, provincial training, NGO training)
- Recognize that mutual respect and understanding, including supporting each other's work, are essential for the development of the commune
- Work together to support each other rather than waiting for instructions or assignments
- Promote gender equality within the commune, e.g. by providing effective gender training
- Integrate gender into commune planning

Outcomes

The FCFs and the councillor network are now recognized throughout Cambodia for having contributed to increasing the capacity of women leaders at the local level, improving their ability to manage their work, and increasing their value in the eyes of male colleagues. Women councillors who have participated say they feel more confident, have better relations with their colleagues, are liaising more with constituents, and that where support from family was lacking, that support has improved. They also report that they have been able to work with other council members to foster a more supportive working environment. As a result of these improvements, women councillors report being assigned more responsible and varied work, such as being appointed to committees dealing with planning, budgeting, procurement, land disputes, women and children's affairs, gender equality, health, civil registration, and information dissemination. Some women councillors have also gained skills in fund raising, and are using the contacts that they have made via the FCFs with NGOs and the private sector to raise money to support projects within their communes, responding to the needs of poor people, especially women. Many also report being involved in resolving disputes within the community, on issues such as domestic violence and land rights. Further, participants said that since the forums began, their opinions were more valued within their councils, and that they felt more able to challenge discrimination.

The success of the FCFs in raising the profile and credibility of women councillors among the electorate in Cambodia can be seen in the results of the commune elections held in April 2007, although of course many other

---

Box 4.2 Pum Hoeun, second deputy of Angcheum commune, Tbaung Khmom district, Kampong Cham province

Fifty-one-year-old Pum Hoeun, a midwife married with two children, was elected at the 2002 elections. Pum Hoeun represents the opposition party, as a result of which she faced considerable hostility from the commune chief, and from some other male commune council members when she was first elected. By attending the forum, Pum Hoeun learned a great deal about how to deal with others, how to communicate effectively, and how to challenge and overcome discrimination. Her hard work, increased confidence, and improved communication skills have led to her being appointed to lead committees on land dispute, domestic violence, women and children's affairs, and commune development planning. She has also established good relations with the police, and says that she can now go to them at any time and ask them to accompany her to help resolve disputes. Pum Hoeun also secured funding for the commune from various NGOs and donors, for projects to build a bridge in the commune, and to provide toilets for individual houses, directly benefiting disadvantaged members of her constituency.

Pum Hoeun is very proud that she has proved herself to be capable; more importantly, she feels a close affinity to all the members of her commune council as well as the people who elected her. As a result of her efforts to serve her community, Pum Hoeun is now respected and valued by her constituents and the political party she represents. Thanks to this, in 2007 she was re-elected to the post of second deputy in her constituency.

factors will also have influenced the increased numbers of women elected. One-thousand six-hundred and fifty-one women were elected as commune councillors (14 per cent of all councillors), of whom 63 were elected as commune chiefs, a considerable improvement on the 34 women elected as commune chiefs in 2002.

Next steps

Eventually, WFP plans to hand over the management and leadership of the FCFs to the women councillors themselves. This has been made clear from the start: during the first two forums, the handover process was explained to participants, and four councillors were chosen in each province by the women councillors to receive training in facilitation skills. These women have worked closely with WFP facilitators to plan and prepare for subsequent forums, and have received detailed feedback at the end of each forum. The handover process is expected to be completed by 2008, by which time subsequent FCFs will be facilitated entirely by the female councillors themselves, with ongoing mentoring and support from WFP.

In addition to handing over the facilitation of FCFs to women councillors, WFP is also working to ensure the future sustainability of this project by integrating the FCF network into existing decentralized local government structures. In early 2007, WFP organized Provincial Round Tables in five provinces, attended by: representatives from provincial and national government; representatives from NGOs working on women's rights and decentralization; district and commune level chiefs; and councillors from three different political parties who had taken part in the FCFs.

The objectives of the Round Tables were:

- to discuss the necessity of specific support interventions for women in public office, and in particular for female councillors;
- to brief participants on the concept of the FCFs;
- to channel the concerns of female councillors to higher levels of government; and
- to discuss modes of co-operation, and to attract further financial and logistical support from Commune Councils, Provincial Local Administration Units (PLAU),[2] the Ministry of Women's Affairs, and the provincial governor and his administration.

As a result of the Provincial Round Tables, the PLAU have committed to take on a greater role in organizing and supporting the FCF. At the Round Table, the Ministry of the Interior also pledged its support for the FCFs, and agreed to cover the expenses of councillors attending the forums, although how this will work has not yet been determined.

Box 4.3 Duch Malin, chief of Yeang commune, Pourk district, Sieam Reap province

Duch Malin is a 46-year-old widow with five children. In 2000 she was elected onto the village development committee, and in 2002 became the only woman councillor among six male colleagues in Yeang commune. Her early experiences as a councillor were not positive, and she often felt like resigning because the male councillors were so hostile towards her.

Attending the FCF has helped Duch Malin to increase her confidence and improve her skills. It gave her the idea of helping a particularly disadvantaged group in her commune – those affected by HIV and AIDS. Many men migrate from Yeang commune to Thailand to work, and often bring HIV back with them. Duch Malin spends time with the families of these migrants, informing them about HIV, and about other livelihood options that do not involve migration. Many people have come to her for help, and she has taken them to get tested for HIV. With the support of an NGO, she has set up a group of volunteers who accompany people to get tested, and take rice donations to people living with HIV or AIDS, orphans, and other poor families. In order to ensure that this support continues, Duch Malin intends to incorporate the project into the next commune plan. Her extensive work in this area has earned her the nickname 'Mother of AIDS'.

In 2007 Duch Malin was re-elected as commune chief. Seeing the importance of the FCF, she has advocated with local authorities at all levels to support the project. At the Provincial Round Table, she called for the provincial governor to include other elected female councillors in the forum, and to invite some male commune chiefs who still lack understanding regarding women's and children's issues. Her recommendation was welcomed by the other participants, and led to the provincial governor pledging to provide financial support to allow more councillors and commune chiefs to attend future forums.

Sum Kalyan, councillor, Damnak Ampil commune, Ang Snoul district, Kandal province

Sum Kalyan is a 42-year-old widow with three children, who was the commune trade officer before being elected in 2002 as the only woman among the five councillors. Her work was appreciated by her political party, colleagues, and by her constituents, but Sum Kalyan found speaking in public or at meetings very difficult. She would tremble every time she tried to speak, even when she had written notes in front of her. At council meetings, when each councillor would be asked to give his or her opinion, when Sum Kalyan could see that her turn was coming up, she would excuse herself and go to the bathroom to wash her face, and wait there until her turn had passed before returning to her seat. She was worried that she would make a mistake, and thought that her opinions were worthless. When she knew she had to make a speech, she would prepare several days in advance, and practise, but when the time came would be too nervous to speak.

Attending the FCF has really helped Sum Kalyan increase her confidence with regards to speaking in public, meaning that she can now contribute far more constructively to council meetings and debates. At the forum, she had plenty of opportunity to speak and make presentations in front of the other participants. 'I now feel more confident. I can speak out in front of people without trembling, sometimes I don't need to write on a piece of paper because I can memorize [what I want to say]. I can challenge my party superior and my male commune council colleagues. I feel like I have 100 spirits that protect me, thanks to the forum.'

Sum Kalyan was re-elected as commune councillor in 2007, and was chosen to be an FCF facilitator for Kandal province. At the Provincial Round Table, Sum Kalyan was brave enough to share her honest ideas and concerns, some of which related to her own commune chief's attitudes and behaviour. Her commune chief, who also attended the Round Table, admitted his lack of understanding and support, and promised to contribute towards her expenses for attending subsequent forums.

Conclusion

The FCF project has been recognized as an important means of enabling women policy makers at the local government level to build confidence and skills, and to gain an awareness of the importance of addressing gender inequality. As such, it has received the support of various government bodies at the national (Ministry of the Interior and Ministry of Women's Affairs), provincial, and local levels. This means that these bodies are now ready to support the continued existence of the FCFs and to enable female councillors to attend them, and that the FCFs will be integrated into the system of decentralized government that now exists in Cambodia.

Many of the councillors who attended the FCFs are now more effective in their roles, particularly regarding their ability to analyse issues relating to women and children, to respond to the needs of their constituencies, and to input into decision-making. It is therefore expected that political parties in Cambodia will make efforts to revise their policies to nominate more women to stand at future elections at both commune and national level.

Through their efforts to respond to the needs of poorer members of their communities, some of which are mentioned in the individual case studies above, the councillors who have participated in the FCFs have also gained the acceptance and respect of their constituents, who now appreciate the contributions that they can make to commune development, and the importance of the equal participation of women and men as witnessed in commune councils. With this important endorsement, it is hoped that women councillors will be even more persuasive and successful in the leadership positions that they now occupy, and will contribute even more constructively to development processes at the local level.

About the author

Menh Navy is Gender Leader for Oxfam GB in Cambodia.

Notes

1. The commune council is the lowest level of local government in Cambodia, directly elected by the Cambodian people. There are five, seven, nine, or eleven members of each commune council, depending on the size of the population and the area that the commune covers. The leader of the commune is called the commune chief.
2. The PLAU is the unit established under the office of the province/municipality to act as a secretariat of the province/municipality governor in the implementation of the decentralization policy.

CHAPTER 5

Breaking the barriers: Sierra Leonean women on the march

Joanna Hoare

Contributors: Kpanja Kutubu-Koroma and Abimbola Akinyemi

Women in Sierra Leone are under-represented in politics and over-represented among poor people. This chapter describes the activities of two projects – the Women In Leadership project and its successor, the Promoting A Culture of Equal Representation project – that have aimed to increase the numbers of women in local and national government. In so doing, they have helped female election candidates to overcome some of the considerable barriers facing them.

Introduction

Situated on the west coast of Africa, Sierra Leone has a population of around 6 million, of whom 52 per cent are women. When Sierra Leone attained independence in 1961, its citizens had high aspirations for their country, which is rich in natural, mineral, and human resources. Women in particular had hopes that with independence, the new regime would promote their rights, and that the discrimination they faced would become a thing of the past.

Unfortunately, this early promise has not yet been realized. Many years of poor governance, corruption, and a lack of respect for human rights led eventually to an 11-year civil war (1990–2001). Women and girls suffered particularly, due to the widespread use of rape and sexual violence as a weapon of war, and the abduction and sexual exploitation of girls by armed forces. Women were made to suffer the consequences of the poor choices of the male-dominated political leadership of Sierra Leone, and they suffered at the hands of the rebels, the male-led perpetrators of the war.

After the war, as calls for disarmament, rehabilitation, reconstruction and peace took centre stage, so did the cry for the increased participation of women in elected leadership. So widespread was the belief that women had as much right to leadership as men, that one of the key recommendations of the Truth and Reconciliation Commission (established to broker the peace process in 2001) was that the government of Sierra Leone should immediately establish a policy on political affirmative action for women.

Despite this recommendation, no affirmative-action policies have yet been put in place, and women continue to be under-represented in Sierra Leonean politics and other mechanisms of decision-making. Barriers to women's political participation are grounded in common beliefs and practices that relate to the role of women. These beliefs limit the spheres within which women can practically or acceptably operate, as well as reinforcing the acceptance of gender-based discrimination and violence. Until quite recently, for example, women were disadvantaged in the customary and common law systems (in relation to family law, property, and inheritance rights in particular). This disadvantage was both an expression of and an influence on the relationships within households, in which the wife and children are typically dependent on male relatives for practically all decisions to do with the welfare of the family.

But if women are under-represented in decision-making, they are over-represented among poor people. According to the country's poverty reduction strategy paper, maternal mortality, infant mortality, and fertility rates in Sierra Leone are among the highest in the world. School attendance and literacy rates are significantly higher among males than females, with very marked imbalances in the eastern and northern regions.[1] The status of women in rural areas is particularly low.

In addition, systems of governance in Sierra Leone are still being re-established. The 2004 local elections marked the first opportunity for Sierra Leoneans to elect local government representatives. The elections also supported a new policy of decentralization, introduced under the Local Government Act (2004). This gave new powers to local authorities, making them responsible for health, education, and other social services. As such, women elected to local government positions are now in a position to make an impact on the design and delivery of those services, with positive repercussions for all women in Sierra Leone. In particular, election to local government could give women an important opportunity to influence local poverty reduction and development policy, to ensure that it meets the particular needs of poor women.

The Women In Leadership (WIL) project

The WIL project was designed by the 50/50 Group, a Sierra Leonean women's rights organization committed to increasing the political participation of women at every level,[2] and Oxfam GB. The aim of the project was to increase the quantity – and quality – of women in local council positions and to ensure that as leaders they would work towards the alleviation of poverty and gender inequality.[3] This was to be achieved by identifying 390 women, one from each council ward in Sierra Leone, and providing them with intense training and support during the election period. In this way, they would be equipped with the skills and confidence to stand in the 2004 local elections, and to be effective representatives in the event of their being elected. It was hoped that of the 390 women, all would stand for election, and at least 100 would be elected.

Training was provided by women who had received election training from 50/50 prior to the 2002 parliamentary and presidential elections; several of the trainers were members of Parliament themselves. The training focused on preparing the would-be candidates for election, and covered campaigning skills, communication skills, information on the workings of representative government, and the principles, rights, and responsibilities of an elected government and its electorate. Candidates also received ongoing support from 50/50 throughout the election period, and were assisted in developing their manifestos and campaign strategy.

The successes

Three hundred and seventy women received the training, of whom 116 aspired to council positions. These would-be candidates represented different political parties, and some were independents. They came from different ethnic backgrounds, representing eight of the ten ethnic groups in Sierra Leone, and most were from poor households and had little formal education. Of the 116, 86 did eventually contest, and 53 were elected (out of a total of 475 councillors). This was far fewer than anticipated. But as the other women who participated in the training were mainly leaders of grassroots women's organizations, community leaders, teachers, and activists, their participation will have had a positive impact on the development of women's leadership at district level. In addition, these participants reported feeling inspired by the training to return to their communities to encourage women to vote in the elections. So their involvement in the training strengthened the participation of women in the electoral process. This was vital in a context where voter ignorance was such that many women did not realize they had the right to *vote*, let alone stand for election.

Women who had participated in the training and went on to stand for election reported that it had strengthened their confidence, both in terms of giving them the courage to stand up and speak on campaign platforms and to challenge intimidation, and in helping them to develop their ideas into a manifesto. Knowing that they had access to ongoing support from 50/50 was also identified as a positive factor that helped them to secure election, as was the support of a good campaign manager, and of family and community members.

While the numbers of women councillors elected was lower than 50/50 and Oxfam GB had hoped, the training and support provided via the WIL project has helped to ensure that the quality of women councillors is higher than it might otherwise have been. Women councillors elected in 2004 are reported to take their responsibilities extremely seriously, seeing themselves as role models who have a duty to 'do a good job' in order to encourage other women to participate in political processes.[4] Likewise, at an evaluation workshop held by 50/50 after the elections, women talking about what had inspired them to stand for election listed factors such as the desire to work with and for the community, to advocate on behalf of marginalized groups in society, and to uphold women's rights to health, education, and shelter.[5] In addition, WIL helped build the capacity of 50/50 itself, providing it with the opportunity to expand beyond the capital Freetown, to recruit many new members, and to raise awareness of its activities.

The challenges

Barriers facing women candidates in Sierra Leone

One significant outcome of the WIL project was the information that it generated regarding the specific barriers to women's political leadership and participation in Sierra Leone. These barriers represented a significant challenge to the project and to the candidates that it sought to support. But the fact that they have now been identified means that in future, projects aiming to improve women's political participation in Sierra Leone can be tailored to overcome them.

Women candidates speaking at the 50/50 evaluation workshop reported that hostile attitudes among men and women towards the very concept of women standing for election was one of the main problems that they faced.[6] These ranged from men stating that they would only ever vote for male candidates, to women passing moral judgement on female candidates, and saying that they should stay at home and attend to their families, rather than trying to assume 'male' positions of leadership. Women members of Parliament and councillors were interviewed for a baseline survey, used to inform the proposal for the next stage of 50/50 and Oxfam GB's work in this field, and they reported similar experiences.[7] The lack of solidarity from women voters was particularly difficult for female candidates, as was the lack of support that many received from members of their own families. Both indicate the need for widespread sensitization of male and female voters, to encourage people to accept that women have the right to enter the political arena, and have vital contributions to make there, for the benefit of all.

Women candidates also identified their *own* lack of confidence and experience as an obstacle to their standing for election, and to fulfilling their duties as councillors once they were elected. Many different factors contribute to this lack of confidence, not least the fear of entering into a 'male' domain where they were likely to face isolation, hostility, and potentially violence.[8] But of more significance for many women candidates was their own lack of education, and limited literacy, particularly when it came to working in English, rather than Krio[9] or their own first language. As well as affecting women's confidence and hence their decision to stand for election, poor literacy skills impact on women councillors' capacity to fulfil their duties if they are elected. This points to the need to provide targeted adult literacy programmes for women who, aside from their lack of education, would make excellent councillors or leaders in other sectors, as well as, of course, providing effective school education for future generations of Sierra Leonean women. Women who were elected to councils also reported that they felt they would benefit from ongoing training, again to boost their confidence and improve their skills, in order to allow them to be more effective representatives.

The inability to raise funds was cited as another barrier to women standing for election. Oxfam GB and 50/50 had different approaches to this. 50/50 decided to allocate a grant of Le 200,000 ($68) to each candidate who had received training, to cover her expenses; Oxfam GB could not endorse this, as it felt that providing funding to candidates compromised the neutrality of the project. These grants were clearly of great assistance however, as many of the candidates said that having access to this money contributed to enabling them to stand for election.[10]

Candidates also reported facing other significant structural barriers, frequently grounded in sexist attitudes regarding the unsuitability of women holding elected office, and in the desire of men to maintain control of the political arena. There was a lack of support from their own political parties, from failing to provide sufficient funding to women candidates, to placing women low down their lists of candidates or replacing them at the last minute with a male candidate. There were even threats, intimidation, and sabotage from male candidates.[11] Candidates also referred to the strong, patriarchal patronage system in Sierra Leone, which gave some male candidates access to political and financial support, compromising their accountability to their less influential constituents in the process.

In addition to the lack of support from their own parties, some women candidates reported that the National Electoral Commission (NEC), the institution organizing the elections, had made their experience of standing for election *more* difficult, rather than easier. Several women who had stood as independent candidates said that NEC officials had refused to register them, and had challenged their right to stand.[12] In addition, it is clear that NEC was not able to fulfil its remit of informing people about their right to vote, and the voting process.[13] NEC officials need to be trained in how to deal with all candidates and voters, male and female, in a professional and gender-sensitive manner.

Project limitations

The main limitation of this project was lack of time. The local elections were announced at very short notice, leaving candidates with just a few months to register and organize their campaigns. For the WIL project, this meant that the training of trainers (who then went on to train candidates) was not held until a few days before the start of the campaign period. This meant that some female candidates who could have benefited from the training did not attend, as they decided to prioritize their campaigns instead. Training materials were adapted from a manual developed by 50/50 and the British Council for the 2002 national elections, and did not cover the decentralization process or the Local Government Act (mainly because information on the latter was not available until too late). This meant that while the training did help the candidates in their campaigning, it did not equip them with the information that they needed to understand the political process in which they were involved, nor make them fully aware of what being a local councillor might involve.[14] This has of course impacted on the capacity of the women councillors to fulfil their responsibilities as elected officials. Supporting and developing the skills of women once elected is an area that, in retrospect, should have formed a far more central aspect of the project than it did. 50/50 and Oxfam GB are both committed to increasing the numbers of women in elected positions in Sierra Leone; it will be difficult to convince the electorate and the government of the merits of this without being able to show that female leaders are just as capable as their male counterparts at fulfilling their responsibilities as elected officials.

In addition to time constraints, the partnership between Oxfam GB and 50/50 was at times difficult, due for the most part to unrealistic expectations on both sides, particularly regarding the capacity of 50/50 to achieve the very ambitious targets set for the WIL project in such a short space of time. More effort could also have been made to target women from a more diverse range of backgrounds to participate in the WIL training (and hence be encouraged to stand for election, or at least play a more active role in mobilizing other women to vote), rather than relying on 50/50's existing contacts.[15]

The lessons

There were many other factors, unrelated to the limitations of the WIL project, that contributed to the low numbers of women elected to local councils in the 2004 elections. Chief among these are the attitudinal and structural barriers to women's full participation in the political arena outlined above, and the widespread acceptance of gender inequality – and gender violence – that underpin them. Perhaps the most salient lesson from this project, then, is that striving to increase the numbers of women in positions of leadership will, on its own, have little impact on women's lives unless the discrimination, poverty, and violence that so many women face in Sierra Leone are also challenged.[16]

That said, there are lessons that have been learned from the design and implementation of the WIL project and which have been incorporated into the next stage of Oxfam GB and 50/50's work promoting women's leadership in Sierra Leone. Two of the most important lessons are the need to allow sufficient time to plan and implement the project, and to ensure that the project is a genuine joint initiative between the two organizations. Closely linked to the latter is the need to make sure that adequate attention is placed on developing the capacity of 50/50 to be an effective champion of women's rights in Sierra Leone.

Another lesson is the importance of identifying would-be candidates who are genuinely committed to their communities, making sure that they have a realistic understanding of what being a local councillor entails, and then providing ongoing support and training to them once they have been elected. Since the elections in 2004, many councillors – male as well as female – have unfortunately not proved themselves to be competent representatives. For some women councillors, this is due to difficulties in combining their work as councillors with their other responsibilities, as well as to a lack of skills, confidence, and experience. Many women councillors reported feeling over-whelmed in their new roles, particularly by the need to operate in English. This makes it difficult for them to contribute during council meetings, as does the fact that when they do, they are often over-ruled by male councillors any-way.[17] Targeted training to help women councillors to be more assertive, and to be able to operate effectively in English, would enable women councillors to fulfil their potential as leaders of their communities, as would materials to prepare them for the role itself (such as training materials on the Local Government Act[18]). However, while carefully designed and targeted training may be useful in building confidence and leadership skills, it should not be invested in at the expense of reducing the structural constraints to women's full and equal participation in political life.[19]

The importance of identifying and mobilizing sympathetic male 'champi-ons' of women's right to leadership is a further lesson learned from the WIL project. Without the support of powerful men in their communities, many women felt that they could not stand as candidates.[20] Where male leaders were supportive, this not only helped some women to get elected in the first place, but has also allowed them to carry out their duties as councillors in a more effective manner. One positive example comes from Makeni town coun-cil. Here, the male council chair recognized that the four female councillors elected in 2004 were less experienced and knowledgeable than other council-lors, so has ensured that they attend classes on the national poverty reduction strategy paper, community education for development, urban management systems, and democracy and finances for local government. He also refuses to make council decisions unless all four female councillors are present at council meetings,[21] which is a clear endorsement of their right to participate in council decision-making and of their ability to do so. However, it is not just a question of 50/50 and Oxfam GB supporting male leaders who have already shown their commitment to women's rights, but also of sensitizing men (and women) at all levels of society to the importance of women's participation in politics and governance, the benefits that this can bring for all in terms of pro-moting inclusive and pro-poor policy, and the fact that women have the *right* to participate, regardless of anything else.[22] This would, hopefully, ensure that women intending to stand for election (or wishing to take up other positions of leadership) had the support of their families and communities, rather than resistance from them.

Finally, an important focus for future work needs to be on enabling women from *all* levels of Sierra Leonean society to attain positions of leadership, in recognition of the vast differences between women in terms of socio-economic status, education, and access to power. Women are not a homogenous group, in Sierra Leone or anywhere else, and it is wrong to assume that a woman elected to office will necessarily represent the interests of other women lower down the social scale. A proactive effort needs to be made to ensure that poorer and otherwise marginalized women are included in any future leadership training and other programme activities,[23] in order that they are then able to contribute to decision-making regarding poverty reduction and development in Sierra Leone. In addition, women already in office need to be encouraged to represent the interests of all their constituents, particularly those at the bottom end of the social spectrum, and to remember that they are accountable to them.

Moving on: promoting a culture of equal representation

The challenges and lessons identified above were taken into careful consideration in the design of the Promoting A Culture of Equal Representation (PACER) project, the next stage of Oxfam GB and 50/50's programme work on women's participation and leadership in Sierra Leone.

The project's first two strategies relate to increasing the numbers of women in Parliament and local councils. Lessons learned from WIL on the need to enable women from all socio-economic levels to attain leadership positions, and to support the capacity of women elected to office to represent their constituencies effectively, will be addressed. Activities include providing tailored training to would-be candidates in public speaking, campaigning, communication, leadership, and fundraising, and encouraging and mobilizing people to support the right of women to stand for office. Women elected at the 2007 national and 2008 local elections will be provided with ongoing mentoring support from 50/50 as well as from experienced female and male representatives from the different levels of government in Sierra Leone. Support will include training in gender analysis (including representing the interests of poor women), participatory planning, and participatory monitoring and evaluation.

In addition to helping women representatives to realize their potential as leaders, it is anticipated that the quality of government in Sierra Leone will improve, and that more generally, this will contribute to the country's development and poverty-reduction strategies. As more women become visible as leaders, it is also hoped that they will act as role models, helping to change attitudes about gender roles, and gender discrimination.

The PACER project's third strategy is to bring the government of Sierra Leone to establish formal mechanisms to promote more equal numbers of women at all levels of government, including introducing a quota for female candidates, in co-operation with other civil-society organizations and networks campaigning for electoral reform in Sierra Leone. It is recognized that for this to occur, other changes must also happen, such as reductions in the official financial requirements for standing for election.

Finally, the project aims to strengthen the capacity of 50/50 to become an effective champion of gender equality in politics and representation through training, human-resource recruitment and development, coaching, fundraising, and strategy development.

Progress so far

The PACER project is ongoing; progress thus far has been encouraging.

50/50 is now firmly established as a national organization, with offices in Freetown and two other districts. Dedicated programme and administrative staff have been recruited, meaning that the organization's activities will no longer be dependent on volunteers. Vital information on the existing barriers to women's participation in Sierra Leone has been collected and this is influencing the work of 50/50 and Oxfam GB, and of other organizations working on similar issues. An example of how this information was used is seen in the development of a training manual for use with candidates standing for the 2007 parliamentary elections.

The numbers of women who did stand for Parliament in 2007 was lower than desired (64), in part because the country moved away from the proportional representation system to constituency-based elections. Under the old system, electors voted for a particular party, rather than for an individual candidate. Constituency-based elections require candidates to carry out face-to-face campaigning. This put women candidates at a disadvantage, partly because it is cost-intensive, and women are less likely to have financial sponsorship, and partly because it means coming into direct contact with resistance at the community level to the very idea of a woman member of Parliament. Of course, this again indicates the ongoing need to encourage people to accept women's rights to political participation. Bringing together community leaders, local council officials, and leaders from women's and youth organizations in order to encourage discussion of issues that particularly affect women and young people has helped reduce this resistance, as has targeting male-led organizations and male community leaders as allies, rather than opponents.

Other significant early successes have been that 50/50 and Oxfam GB have managed to ensure that, prior to the 2007 elections, NEC produced new voter education materials that were gender-sensitive. One hundred and sixty-four electoral officials across the country were trained to be more gender-aware in their work during the election period, and to take into account the different needs of women candidates and voters. In addition, 50/50 has successfully formed an alliance with other like-minded organizations to challenge the national government and political parties to review policies on women, including considering the introduction of quotas for women in government.

About the author

Joanna Hoare wrote this chapter while working for Oxfam GB. She now works as a freelance editor and writer on gender and development issues.

Notes

1. Government of Sierra Leone (2000) 'Status of Women and Children in Sierra Leone: A Household Survey Report', (Multi Indicator Cluster Surveys), Freetown: Government of Sierra Leone.
2. 50/50 was founded in 2000 with the aim of increasing women's participation in democratic politics and other decision-making processes. It seeks to achieve this through changing public perceptions of women in politics, encouraging and empowering women to seek and hold public office, and lobbying for equal numbers of men and women in political representation.
3. The WIL project actually consisted of two components, the first of which was to build the capacity of women's organizations, and the second of which was to increase the numbers of women elected. This chapter describes the second component.
4. M. Harding (2005) 'Evaluation Report of Component Two of the Women In Leadership Project'.
5. 50/50 Group (2004) 'Report of the Post-Local Government Elections Assessment Workshop', Freetown: 50/50 Group.
6. *Ibid.*
7. 50/50 Group and Oxfam (2006) 'Equal Representation (PACER) Project Baseline Survey Report', Freetown: 50/50 Group and Oxfam.
8. *Ibid.*
9. Krio is more widely spoken as a second language throughout Sierra Leone than English, and acts as a 'lingua franca'. See http://en.wikipedia.org/wiki/Krio_language (last accessed September 2007).
10. M. Harding *op.cit.*; C. Roseveare (2006) 'Review of Oxfam Sierra Leone Women In Leadership (WIL) Project, Some Learning and Recommendations'; 50/50 Group *op.cit.*
11. 50/50 Group and Oxfam *op.cit.*; Roseveare *op.cit.*
12. M. Harding *op.cit.*
13. M. Harding *op.cit.*; C. Roseveare *op.cit.* To be fair, NEC was convened and asked to organize the elections at very short notice.
14. C. Roseveare *op.cit.*
15. M. Harding *op.cit.*; C. Roseveare *op.cit.*
16. C. Roseveare *op.cit.*
17. C. Roseveare *op.cit.*; M. Harding *op.cit.*
18. M. Harding *op.cit.*
19. C. Roseveare *op.cit.*
20. *Ibid.*
21. M. Harding *op.cit.*
22. 50/50 Group and Oxfam *op.cit.*; 50/50 Group *op.cit.*
23. M. Harding *op.cit.*

CHAPTER 6

Raising voices: training for empowerment for women experiencing poverty in Britain

Sue Smith

Contributors: Louise Falconer, Nikki van der Gaag, and Zoe Smith

> *The UK may be a developed country, but almost 25 per cent of the population live below the poverty line. Women experience higher levels of poverty than men, just as they do in other parts of the world. Encouraging and supporting poor women to voice their own experiences and speak out to challenge the inequality that they face are vital to overcoming poverty in the UK. Recognizing this, Oxfam GB has worked with partner organizations to enable women to meet with and lobby the civil servants and politicians who make decisions that impact on their lives*

Background

Oxfam GB set up its UK Poverty Programme in the mid-1990s. Right from the start, the decision was taken to focus on gender inequality. This is because even in such a rich country, women are more likely than men to experience poverty at some point in their lives.[1] Single women pensioners are more likely than single men pensioners to live in poverty in retirement.[2] A combination of factors including occupational segregation and the fact that women are more likely than men to be in part-time work, due to unpaid caring responsibilities, means that women's incomes are on average lower than men's.[3] And women bringing up children on their own find it hard to afford child-care to enable them to go out to work.

Women's poverty in the UK is often caused not by direct discrimination against women, but by the fact that many women's life paths do not fit the pay and reward systems of organizations, or the way in which pensions and other state benefits are earned. For instance, women are more likely than men to take periods of time out of paid employment in order to have and bring up children, which has an impact on their National Insurance[4] and pension contributions and thus their entitlements to state benefits. While girls have the same educational opportunities as boys, and often do better at school, once they leave school, economically disadvantaged girls (and the women they become) come face-to-face not only with gender-related structural barriers which may limit opportunities available to them to enter paid employment and access state benefits, but also gendered assumptions about what they can and cannot do. These assumptions, along with the low levels of confidence that many women living in poverty experience, are as hard to overcome in the UK as they are anywhere else in the world.

Understanding this context makes it easier to see why building poor women's confidence to challenge their economic position, and the structures and forces keeping them there, is an important anti-poverty measure. From the start, Oxfam GB's programme in Wales, the north of England, and Scotland, saw the importance of building women's confidence to help them recognize how the structures of society and the economy keep them in poverty, and to tackle the situation to their own advantage through lobbying for changes to the policies that uphold this structural inequality. Unless women can take a lead, individually or together, nothing will ever change, even in such a developed country.

In this chapter we reflect on what approaches Oxfam GB has found successful in the UK, what has not worked so well, and what we have learned about how to support women's participation and engagement with providers of public services.

Raising women's voices at the local and national level

Creating space for equal participation

Women's lives are busy and the unpaid caring roles that many women undertake mean they are less likely to be able to enter the public arena than men. We also believe that gender stereotyping has as much influence on women's own perceptions of their abilities to participate in decision-making processes, and on general assumptions regarding whether or not women make 'good' leaders in the UK, as it does in the developing world, and that tackling this will take many years. In light of these realities, Oxfam GB's UK programme is based on the belief that the following things need to take place in order to create the space for poor women's equal participation:

- decision-makers need to be sensitized to the need to listen to women at the local level, especially those living below the poverty line[5] or those living in poor communities (this will lead to policies that draw on these women's insights and experiences and the knowledge that they have of how poverty affects their communities);
- women experiencing poverty need to make their voices heard with decision-makers, and learn how to lobby; and
- women need to be prepared to become decision-makers themselves.

Oxfam GB's work on women's leadership

With the aims identified above in mind, Oxfam GB and our partners have worked on a range of projects using different methods to support women's participation and leadership. These include the 'Engendering Change' project, which focuses on building women's political understanding of who decision-makers are at both local and national levels in their political context, and strengthens their capacity and skills to influence those decision-makers.[6] Elsewhere, working through the ReGender Project, Oxfam GB has piloted capacity-building for women in urban areas experiencing regeneration.[7]

In addition to the projects above, Oxfam GB has worked on two projects that have enabled women to gain a greater understanding of the structures that sustain gender inequality and keep them in poverty. The two projects – one focusing on economic literacy and empowerment in Scotland, the other a participatory research project on women's experiences of poverty – have helped participants to challenge those structures by voicing their own experiences, and their demands, to civil servants and politicians at the local and national level. This chapter discusses lessons learned from these two projects.

Working at the local level: 'Women's Economic Empowerment' project

In 2006–2007 Oxfam in Scotland ran a series of training courses on women's economic empowerment, in collaboration with local agencies in three deprived areas in Scotland: South Lanarkshire, Dundee, and Inverclyde. The courses were intended to build women's confidence to think about their futures, to bring out their experiences of paid work and their views on local services such as transport and housing, and to provide an opportunity for them to voice their experiences to a local job-support agency (Routes to Work South) and to local service providers. The courses ran for two days a week for four weeks, and participants were recruited by Oxfam GB staff working in those areas. The courses were facilitated by someone with extensive experience working on empowerment projects. The sessions began with the women discussing a short film which dealt with direct discrimination. From this, they went on to look at power, how it operates, and what impact it has on experiences and opportunities. This analysis of power and its impact is something that is frequently missing from training with women living in deprivation in the UK.

None of the participants was in paid work, but almost all had a strong desire to work outside the home. All experienced significant barriers in entering the labour market, such as the need for flexible hours, or the problem of low self-esteem. Oxfam GB staff went out to find and recruit the poorest women in the community, who did not usually attend such events. The women on the women's economic empowerment training in Larkhall, South Lanarkshire, spoke of the sessions as 'lighting up so many lightbulbs for me' and helping them to '[learn] to stand up and be counted and not just blend into the background'.

Working at the national level: 'Women's Voices of Experience' project

In England in 2006, Oxfam GB worked with the UK Women's Budget Group (WBG) on a participatory research project with women living in poverty. The aims were to involve women in exploring their experiences of poverty, to bring out what they thought the solutions might be, to give them training in how policy making at national level worked, and to build their confidence and skills to meet civil servants and influence them to incorporate their views and experiences into public policy. The WBG contacted 12 local women's organizations providing information, advice, and support to women in the English Midlands, in London, and in Wales. It brought a total of 47 women together for training, and supported their attendance at a seminar in London to meet civil servants from the UK Government Treasury and Department for Work and Pensions, and members of Parliament.

The first phase was an opportunity for women to map their regional experiences of living in poverty. They discussed their individual experiences, and from this drew comparisons that allowed them to then articulate their collective needs. The second phase brought women from the regions together to understand better how decisions are made at the level of national government. This covered basic government structure, and some of the factors which influence decision-making. There were two strands for discussion: one focused on women's experiences of claiming state financial support, and the other had a broader focus which the women chose themselves. The themes they raised included isolation, children, and child-care; employment and education; physical and mental health; and the 'postcode lottery'.[8] The women involved felt a real sense of solidarity having worked in this way.

Lessons learned

Poor women need extra practical and financial support

It cannot be emphasized enough that poor women need extra support to get their voices heard in any kind of public arena. In the first place, they are often not part of established networks to receive information, such as community newsletters or playgroup and nursery notice boards. Recognizing this, in the Women's Economic Empowerment project in Scotland, Oxfam GB recruited participants by word of mouth, as well as via regular community notices. To ensure that their participation was as convenient and as low-cost as possible, the women were given attendance bonus vouchers for £50 negotiated by Oxfam GB with South Lanarkshire Council. In addition, they were collected and taken home by taxi, child-care was arranged and paid for, and lunch was provided. The course was scheduled to fit in with school hours and was intensive, yet did not interfere with the qualifying hours for their state benefits.[9] Oxfam GB knows from experience that these methods work in ensuring the participation of women whose family and financial situation would otherwise prevent them from being involved.

The Voices of Experience project identified key organizations working with women living in poverty, and co-operated with them to identify women who would be interested in participating. Arrangements for support with travel and child-care were also made, but the project's wider geographical spread (Wales, the English Midlands, and London) meant that for some of the women, travelling to London to meet civil servants and staying overnight felt like too big a time commitment. Others who could arrange child-care for this length of time felt it was a welcome break. The ethical guidelines for the project recognized that women should be invited in pairs or with a project worker rather than being expected to come alone, so that they did not feel isolated and unsupported. Payment for their voluntary time spent on the project, whether in meetings or travel, both for the women themselves and for the facilitating organizations, was an issue addressed with only partial success. While the participants were paid for their time, the organizations involved in setting up and running the meetings felt that insufficient funding had been allocated to them, given the amount of time needed to organize these events.

Building solidarity among women

Our experience of working with established or nascent women's groups across the UK has taught us that we cannot assume that women have any sense of shared solidarity. This is partly because discrimination against women is less visible than in other countries, and also because feminism is now labelled in the public mind as old fashioned and extreme. Many women we have worked with see calls for gender equality as '1970s bra-burning', and see no need to get together as women. In the ReGender project mentioned above, one of the dawning realizations for the newly formed groups set up to learn about gender and to lobby regeneration decision-makers was the need to ask the question: what are the men doing in our community? They learnt that as women they had barriers and issues in common, but also recognized that they were very active in unpaid community activities such as organizing child-care and events for young people, and adult education. They also realized that on the whole, men were not participating in these activities. In North Wales, the women then went to men they knew, and asked the question: why don't men help? As one of them said, some men are just as involved as women in looking after children, and taking them to and from school, and jobs around the house, so why are they not involved in the community? Some of the men approached did join the community activities planned.

Challenging gender stereotyping

In Britain, as in the rest of the world, gender stereotyping is a significant factor in determining women's (and men's) ideas about who they are, and what activities are appropriate for them to do. The Equal Opportunities Commission[10] in Scotland recently concluded a study of occupational segregation which showed that women will readily train to be child-care assistants (poorly paid) but rarely consider becoming mechanics (better paid).[11] To try and challenge this, Oxfam in Scotland has worked with council officers in South Lanarkshire who provide careers advice to girls and boys at school. These officers were unaware that the advice they offered channelled girls into poorly paid and stereotypically 'female' jobs such as shop work or hairdressing, and boys into better paid ones such as carpentry or plumbing, or other apprenticeships, until it was brought to their attention by the Oxfam GB staff member who sat in on careers advice for boys and girls. Once this was pointed out to them, many welcomed the realization, and have tried to change the way that they respond to clients as a result.

Helping women to raise their voices

Not only do women need to have the confidence to believe that they have something to contribute, that they *can* make other choices, and that decision-makers need to hear about their experience, they also have to be encouraged to make that contribution.

The capacity-building work with women has been very effective in helping women gain confidence, helping them to understand that their problems are often created by structures and are not their personal fault, and that they are not alone, and helping them to understand how policy is made.

In the Women's Economic Empowerment project in Scotland, the facilitator made a point of starting the training with a discussion of the nature of power and influence. From this the women understood that power was an issue, and they needed to engage with it. Not only did they come to see that many of the problems they faced were due to their own lack of power to make life choices, but also that they found it difficult to challenge others who were in positions of power. For instance, in Larkhall, one of the areas targeted in the project, women realized that they could challenge their children's schools to provide inclusive school outings that do not stigmatize the poorest children who cannot go because their parents are not able to pay. Feeling able to challenge individuals who run services for their children was a real step forward for these women in terms of their confidence and skills, as was the opportunity to put their views strongly to the local job-advice centre.

In the Women's Voices of Experience project, participants recorded their experiences and thoughts by writing them down on pieces of coloured paper. These messages were then fitted together like a patchwork quilt, in a way that built the women's sense of being connected, and reinforced their sense that they had issues in common. The women highlighted not only their entitlement to a decent income, but also their rights to respect and dignity through the unpaid contributions they made to society.

Encouraging the powerful to listen to poor women?

There are two sides to empowerment: building the confidence and skills of people in powerless positions, and ensuring that they are able to occupy a position where they can talk on relatively equal terms to those people with power to make decisions that affect their lives. This chapter has described attempts to do the former: we still have a lot to learn about how to do the latter. We need to spend as long preparing the ground with decision-makers so that they are able to listen, as we do building the skills and confidence of women so that they feel they can speak up. It is a delicate balance: bringing women face to face with decision-makers who then do not treat them seriously can make them feel disempowered, or angry, or both. In the projects described here, Oxfam GB has attempted to prepare both sides prior to meeting, to make those meetings as constructive as possible. But this has had mixed results.

As part of a wider project in Scotland to influence council officers and decision-makers to mainstream gender in service delivery, Oxfam GB worked with Routes to Work South, a local job-advice service in South Lanarkshire. This went some way towards preparing the ground for Routes to Work South to 'hear' what the women were saying about their needs and experiences, during sessions organized as part of the Women's Economic Empowerment project, making it a fairly positive experience for the women who took part. Because the women knew Routes to Work South as a local agency, and knew what they did in the neighbourhood, they could make suggestions in the knowledge of how this would impact on services affecting women like them. Likewise, in Oxfam GB's earlier 'Get Heard' project, a series of meetings between civil servants and anti-poverty organizations established the principles of effective participation (giving it time, providing financial support to people experiencing poverty to enable them to participate, actually listening to participants, and following this up with action) before the project began. Because this led civil servants to have a better understanding of *how* to listen to people, the consultation was wider and more successful than it might have been, and some of the priorities identified by people experiencing poverty were incorporated into the UK National Plan on Social Inclusion, 2006.

In the Women's Voices of Experience project, WBG members were able to contact civil servants and members of Parliament whom they knew, and to persuade them to meet the women. Unfortunately, several of the members of Parliament who promised to come pulled out at the last minute, creating much disappointment. Such is the nature of lobbying the world over, but for women with no experience of this type of work, it felt like a snub. The women also became aware that while civil servants found the experience of meeting them face to face a rewarding one, the gap between what is politically achievable in changes to the benefits system, and what the women felt was necessary to alleviate poverty, is wide, and seemingly difficult to overcome.

Conclusion: Oxfam GB's ongoing role in the UK

So what does Oxfam GB have to offer in promoting women's leadership in the UK, and is it sustainable? Some of the answers to these questions are connected to the position of Oxfam GB's UK Poverty Programme in relation to other anti-poverty organizations and agencies active in the UK.

Women and local officials involved in projects are often surprised, but very appreciative, to learn that Oxfam GB is not involved in this work in order to 'tick boxes', and does not just seek short-term results. We are able to provide resources on a small scale, with no conditions, on terms which the women set themselves. While our projects in the UK are relatively small, we can give sustained and flexible support.

That said, we continue to ask ourselves questions about the sustainability of this work, both for us and for the partners we support. In the UK, compared with other organizations and agencies, we have relatively few resources, but where we are able to add value, and have staff already on the ground, Oxfam GB's work can have a longer-term impact. For instance, in the Women's Economic Empowerment project, we worked in three areas of Scotland, in which Oxfam GB staff members were already engaged and where we already had connections with other organizations and an established record of working on gender in regeneration areas. Another challenge that we and our partners face is that building the capacity of women at the local level is resource-intensive. For instance, the WBG, as a network of women interested in policy and gender analysis, found that they were unprepared for the degree and intensity of support needed not just for the women, but also for the partner organizations with whom they worked on the Voices of Experience project.

We will be monitoring the results of the projects described to establish more clearly whether we are contributing to real long-term change in encouraging women's participation and getting them into positions of leadership. However, we expect to continue working with women for their advancement in economic and political leadership, as we believe this to be at the core of tackling women's poverty in Britain.

About the author

Sue Smith is Senior Policy and Programme Advisor for the UK Poverty Programme, Oxfam GB.

Notes

1. Women's Budget Group (2005) 'Women's and children's poverty: making the links', www.wbg.org.uk/documents/WBGWomensandchildrenspoverty.pdf (last accessed November 2007).
2. New Policy Institute (n.d.), 'The Poverty Site', www.poverty.org.uk (last accessed November 2007).

3. New Policy Institute *ibid.*; Women and Equality Unit (n.d.) 'What is the pay gap and why does it exist?', www.womenandequalityunit.gov.uk/pay/pay_facts.htm (last accessed November 2007).
4. In the UK, everyone in paid employment contributes part of his or her income to the National Insurance scheme. In return, people are entitled to state benefits. Some of these, such as free health care under the National Health Service, and child benefit, are available to everyone, regardless of how many National Insurance contributions they have made. Others, including pensions, are dependent on how many contributions someone has made over the course of his or her life.
5. This 'poverty line' is not the same as a comprehensive definition of poverty. As in other developed countries, poverty is a complex issue in the UK, relating not just to individuals' and families' capacity to access income, but also to their capacity to access credit, or to save for the future. For more information visit www.oxfamgb.org/ukpp/poverty/thefacts.htm (last accessed September 2007).
6. For more information about the Engendering Change project, and Oxfam's partner organization Engender, please see www.oxfamgb.org/ukpp/equal/engenderingchange.htm (last accessed November 2007).
7. Regeneration projects, usually funded by government, renew buildings, roads, public facilities, and communities that are run down and poor. Poor women rarely have any influence over how these projects are planned and delivered. The ReGender project built women's sense of solidarity and recognition that they have issues in common. It has supported women in three areas in Glasgow, Llandudno, and Manchester to lobby local decision makers for their needs to be recognized and considered in urban design and the delivery of public services, such as employment support, transport, and economic development. For more information on this, please see www.oxfam.org.uk/resources/ukpoverty/oxfamswork.html (last accessed December 2007).
8. 'Postcode lottery' is a phrase used to describe the uneven provision of public services in the UK, whereby the services provided in poor areas are fewer and of poorer quality, and people living in these areas feel they are looked down upon, and that service providers treat them with less respect.
9. In Britain people claiming state benefits are allowed to work for up to 16 hours a week without losing their entitlement to payments such as income support from the government.
10. The Equal Opportunities Commission was originally established to monitor the implementation of the Sex Discrimination Act (1975) and the Equal Pay Act (1970). It is now the leading agency challenging sex discrimination and gender inequality in the UK. It has recently been subsumed into the new Commission for Equality and Human Rights (www.eoc.org.uk).
11. EOC Scotland (2006) 'Occupational segregation in Scotland – progress report', Glasgow: EOC Scotland, available at www.eoc.org.uk/PDF/Occ_seg_in_Scotland_progress_report_1_Aug_2006.pdf (last accessed October 2007).

CHAPTER 7

Women's leadership in economic change in the Occupied Palestinian Territories and Israel

Joanna Hoare

Contributors: Catherine Hine and Jamal Atamneh

Arab-Israeli women are one of the most marginalized and invisible groups within Israeli society. Many have been adversely affected by the 'Wisconsin Plan', a welfare-to-work programme introduced by the Israeli government in 2005, that Oxfam's partner, Sawt el-Amel, has been active in opposing. In response to the hardship that the plan has brought to themselves and their families, women have become active in leading popular opposition to the Plan. This is a significant and unprecedented move in their conservative communities, where women's presence in the public sphere has traditionally not been accepted.

Background

The Arab minority in Israel are among the poorest and most marginalized within Israeli society. In addition to high levels of unemployment, many have little education, and access to basic services is limited.[1] The number of Arab women registered as 'unemployed' is particularly high, for two reasons. Women who identify themselves as housewives, and who live in households that are dependent on benefits, have to register as unemployed, even though they may be fully occupied with household responsibilities and looking after children. If they fail to do so, their husbands will also lose access to benefits, putting the welfare of the whole family in jeopardy. And Arab women who do want to enter the job market face a range of obstacles, from low levels of education and professional skills and a poor command of Hebrew, to a lack of demand for female Arab workers, and inadequate public transport, making it very difficult for them to travel to work.[2] These barriers are compounded by gender norms that see women's role as confined to the home, making it very difficult for women to be active in public life.

The Wisconsin Plan

In the context of high levels of unemployment within the Arab community, as well as elsewhere in Israel, in 2005 the Israeli government introduced a new job-placement programme for the 'chronically unemployed', known as the Wisconsin Plan.[3] The Plan is implemented by private employment agencies, and currently affects 14,000 households in Ashkelon, Jerusalem, Hadera, and Nazareth/Upper Nazareth. The dual aims of the project are to help those who have been without work for a long time back into employment, and out of poverty, and to cut public spending on welfare benefits by 35 per cent: the companies running the programme face sanctions if they do not succeed in doing this. People receiving state unemployment benefits in areas where the programme is being implemented now *have* to attend the Wisconsin Plan centres for up to 40 hours a week, and they *have* to accept any job offered to them by the employment agencies, or participate in voluntary work. Anyone who fails to do so loses the right to claim benefits. If a family is dependent on state benefits, both spouses have to attend, even if one is fully occupied caring for young children at home.[4] As women are far more likely to be in this position, they are being disproportionately affected by the scheme.

Challenging an exploitative system

Sawt el-Amel (the Laborer's Voice) was established in 1999 by Arab workers from Nazareth. Its aim is to support low-income and unemployed Arab-Israeli citizens experiencing discrimination in the labour market and the welfare system. This is achieved through a range of activities including collective and individual legal action, advocacy, and campaigns raising awareness about employment and welfare issues among the Arab-Israeli population.[5] Concerns that the implementation of the Wisconsin Plan was having an adverse effect on Arab-Israeli citizens prompted Sawt el-Amel to open an 'Alternative Wisconsin Centre', established with the support of Oxfam GB. This provides information and legal services to people affected by the scheme, helping them to find decent work outside the framework of the Wisconsin Plan, and undertakes advocacy work as well.[6]

Participatory needs assessment (PNA)

The establishment of the Alternative Wisconsin Centre brought Sawt el-Amel activists into contact with both men and women affected by the Wisconsin Plan, and made them realize that they needed more specific information about how the Plan was impacting on women. In light of this, and the fact that women made up the majority of Wisconsin Plan participants,[7] Sawt el-Amel applied to Oxfam GB for funding to carry out a participatory needs assessment (PNA). The PNA would help them to find out more about women's experiences of the Wisconsin Plan, in order to provide more targeted assistance to their women clients, to inform advocacy work, and by extension prevent the exploitation of Arab women by Wisconsin Centres and employers.[8]

As part of the PNA, Sawt el-Amel organized meetings and focus groups for women and men to discuss their concerns and experiences relating to specific topics, such as health rights and the Wisconsin Plan, and children and the Wisconsin Plan. Women Wisconsin Plan participants also spoke to people attending the Wisconsin Centres, reporting back to Sawt el-Amel on their conversations. Coming into contact with these women in this way encouraged more people to visit Sawt el-Amel's Alternative Wisconsin Centre, where staff were able to collect 100 testimonies from people affected by the Plan.[9]

As anticipated, the results of the PNA showed that women were particularly vulnerable to exploitation within the Wisconsin Plan framework. Women's lack of formal education, experience of public life, and familiarity with the benefits system were, Sawt el-Amel argues, exploited by the Wisconsin Centres, where women clients often faced verbal harassment and humiliation.[10] A year into working with women Wisconsin Plan participants, Sawt el-Amel stated that in Nazareth, it could not report a single successful case of a woman participant obtaining decent employment via the scheme.[11] Some women were sent as day labourers to kibbutzim,[12] and had to work in very harsh conditions, for which they were never actually paid. This had the knock-on effect of workers who were already employed as labourers being dismissed, as it was cheaper for employers to use Wisconsin participants. Some women were offered shift work in factories that they could not reach by public transport in time to start work at the beginning of their shifts, and were classed as 'refusing to work' and denied access to benefits when they explained this.[13] The authorities were forced to pay the withheld benefits to these women when Sawt el-Amel appealed on their behalf. Others were not offered any work, because there simply was none available, and yet they were still expected to attend the Wisconsin Centre on a regular basis. When women refused to co-operate, they faced sanctions, principally denial of state benefits. Talking to Sawt el-Amel was seen as a form of 'non-co-operation', effectively obstructing the rights of Wisconsin Plan participants to access support and legal advice. Indeed, 15 women who took part in a protest at one of the Wisconsin Centres had their benefits cut as a result; lawyers instructed by Sawt el-Amel appealed on behalf of these women, and their benefits were reinstated.[14]

One issue identified by many of the women who participated in the PNA was the failure of the Wisconsin Plan to make any allowances for people with young children. Some of the women who were participating in the Wisconsin Plan were registered as unemployed and wanted to find paid employment, but over 60 per cent of women respondents did not actually classify themselves as 'unemployed', but rather as housewives, whose primary role was to take care of their children, but who were part of households reliant on state benefits. These women were still expected to attend the Wisconsin Centre 'full-time', for up to 40 hours a week, and to take any employment offered to them; failure to do so could mean jeopardizing the entire household's access to benefits.[15]

As no child-care facilities were provided, women often had to leave children unattended while they visited the Centre or went out to work, potentially putting their children's safety at risk. Many women also felt guilty that they were not fulfilling their responsibilities towards their children, which they considered their primary role. For some, this was very disempowering, as they associated it with losing the authority and status that they enjoyed within the home as mothers.[16] That said, this emphasis on motherhood and their responsibilities within the home did not mean that women were not committed to bringing about socio-economic change for themselves and their families, and many saw participating in the PNA as a means of being proactively involved in doing just that.[17]

Women leaders: moving from passivity to action

The Women's Platform

Some of the women who gave their views during the PNA decided that they wanted to do more to measure the impact of the Wisconsin Plan on women in particular, and to provide assistance to other women affected by the Plan. Together they formed the 'Women's Platform' in September 2005, which now has five permanent active members (four of whom have been through the Wisconsin Plan themselves), as well as over 40 other members who are involved in the Platform's activities. Working closely with the Popular Committee against the Wisconsin Plan, an independent monitoring body facilitated by Sawt el-Amel, the Women's Platform has a presence at the two Wisconsin Centres in Nazareth. This means that members are able to provide moral support, legal advice, and general information to women affected by the Plan, as well as collecting information from those women about their experiences. The Women's Platform has been able to reach over 3,000 women in this way, collecting comprehensive information that has been used to inform Sawt el-Amel's campaigning and advocacy work, as well as referring individual women in need of specific legal advice to Sawt el-Amel's legal clinic. This has resulted in Sawt el-Amel winning a number of important test cases on behalf of women workers.[18] In addition, lobbying informed by the Women's Platform and its members' experiences of the Wisconsin Plan has resulted in legislated changes to the Plan, meaning in particular that unemployed single women with children under the age of 12 are now no longer expected to attend the Wisconsin Centre full-time.[19]

The first demonstrations against the Plan were led by men, but members of the Women's Platform have become more and more actively involved in organizing public demonstrations, gradually assuming leadership of the public struggle against the Wisconsin Plan.[20] This has included members of the Women's Platform organizing and participating in sit-ins at Wisconsin Centres and a demonstration to mark International Women's Day in 2006; requesting Sawt el-Amel to organize workshops and lectures on the Wisconsin

Plan and workers' rights in relation to it; and speaking at conferences held in Israel, and abroad.[21]

The fact that the women active in Sawt el-Amel's Women's Platform have succeeded in attaining prominent positions of leadership within the campaign against the Wisconsin Plan is extremely significant. Arab-Israeli society is traditionally very patriarchal, with women's mobility and activity outside the home closely controlled by male relatives, leaving women for the most part marginalized and invisible in any public activities. This is compounded by the discrimination that they face from the Israeli state and the general public.[22] But in addition to their anger at the way the Plan has exploited those expected to participate, women are also angered by the fact that women with children are being forced out of their homes, in what is seen as an attack on the home and the family, the foundations of many women's sense of who they are and where their responsibilities lie. Their contact with the Women's Platform has helped them realize that they have the right, and indeed the responsibility, to take action against the scheme and the harm it is doing to their families and communities.[23] In so doing, the enormous potential of these women to bring about positive change as leaders in their communities has been unlocked, and they have shown an unexpected degree of motivation and determination.[24] At an individual level, Sawt el-Amel report that there is a noticeable difference in the way that women who are involved in the Platform's activities perceive themselves; they now have the skills and self-confidence to stand up for their own and their families' rights in public.[25]

Changing power relations

The support that the women active in Sawt el-Amel have received from the men in their community is also noteworthy. Initially some male relatives did try to prevent women from attending meetings and demonstrations, using the excuse that this might mean that they would be singled out as troublemakers and be penalized by Wisconsin Centre staff, potentially losing access to benefits.[26] But on the whole, men have come to be very supportive of the women's activism, with many ultimately agreeing to take part in events organized and led by the Women's Platform,[27] an 'unprecedented social revolution' in terms of gender relations in Arab-Israeli society.[28] Men in the community (and in Sawt el-Amel itself) seem to have realized, and to appreciate, the benefits of women's shared participation in the struggle against the Wisconsin Plan, particularly relating to shared common interests such as the right to decent work, and the welfare of children, and now welcome the leadership of women in that struggle as well.[29] Indeed, the Women's Platform is now fully integrated into the leadership structure of Sawt el-Amel, with members representing the organization at external conferences and events, including events outside of Israel. It is also the most active branch of the Alternative Wisconsin Centre.[30]

The effect of women campaigning on the Wisconsin Plan has been to achieve changes in gender power relations in these communities, but this has happened almost without men noticing. Indeed, it can be argued that the Women's Platform has been so successful in motivating women to act, and in maintaining men's support for that action, precisely because it has never sought to overtly challenge existing ideas about gender roles and relations in Arab-Israeli society.[31] Rather, it has been able to show the benefits to the whole community, men included, of women's activism and their increased role in public life, and it is through recognizing and appreciating these benefits that men have begun to demonstrate that they have altered their views on how women and men should behave.

For instance, no discussion was initiated by Sawt el-Amel regarding whether men taking on more responsibility for child-care would be one solution to the difficulties faced by women participating in the Wisconsin Plan,[32] but it is clear that some 'renegotiation' and redistribution of gender roles and responsibilities must have taken place within the households of these new women activists, in order for them to have the time to participate in this activism on a regular basis, and to travel to attend conferences and events. In particular, the attendance of Women's Platform members at trade-union conferences held in Belgium and France could not have happened without some shift in men's attitudes and power relations occurring within those women's households.[33]

At present such conclusions may be speculative, and the issue of how far women's public participation in resistance to the Wisconsin Plan has altered gendered power relations within households would be an interesting topic for future investigation. However, that women are now taking responsibility for themselves, their husbands, and their children in the public sphere and that men are respecting and even encouraging their right to do so, is, in the words of a senior staff member at Sawt el-Amel, little short of 'revolutionary', given the context in which this has taken place.[34] And the fact that men do not feel threatened by this indicates that these changes are likely to be sustained, although this will need to be monitored in the long run. As a strategy for bringing about change, it is debatable whether prompting a direct discussion on existing gender roles would have been anywhere near as effective.

Further leadership development training

It has become clear that members of the Women's Platform are now the driving force behind social activism against the Wisconsin Plan. Their determination and commitment has enabled them to attain key leadership positions within Sawt el-Amel, with several now active on the organization's steering committee. This is a major change for the organization. As Sawt el-Amel's director put it, five years ago, having women active on the Steering Committee of the organization would have been unthinkable.[35] The fact that they are now in this position indicates the degree to which women's activities against the Wisconsin Plan have challenged gendered power relations within this community.

Being active on the Steering Committee allows Women's Platform members to contribute to the strategic development of Sawt el-Amel, ensuring that further projects aimed specifically at women are developed, and that a gender perspective is integrated into Sawt el-Amel's overall programme.[36] As such, the Women's Platform is now in a position to consider activities that support people affected by the Wisconsin Plan, and potentially address the more general socio-economic vulnerability and lack of economic independence of Arab-Israeli women, through for instance exploring opportunities for income generation and skills development, and addressing the issue of lack of access to reliable public transport.[37] Other activities will include ongoing community activism, providing legal support in individual cases, and developing alliances with other organizations which can advocate for change from outside Israel.[38]

Recognizing that activism against the Wisconsin Plan unlocked enormous potential in the women participants, but that these activists still needed training and support to develop their leadership skills to operate in public and professional environments,[39] the Women's Platform of Sawt el-Amel with support from Oxfam GB launched a 'Grassroots Women's Leadership Development' project. This has provided the opportunity for Arab-Israeli women to develop the skills to stand up for their rights, advocate on behalf of themselves and their families and communities, and become effective leaders. It is hoped that this will eventually lead to a greater number of Arab women active in the public sphere as formal and informal leaders and spokespersons, increasing the visibility of Arab women in Israeli society, and helping, ultimately, to improve their socio-economic status and economic independence.[40] The determination of the members of the Women's Platform has sparked off a new wave of social activism, led by those who are among the most vulnerable in Arab-Israeli society; Sawt el-Amel is committed to supporting this, in order to help it to grow and flourish.

About the author

Joanna Hoare wrote this chapter while working for Oxfam GB. She now works as a freelance editor and writer on gender and development issues.

Notes

1. Sawt el-Amel: The Laborer's Voice (2006a) 'Arab Women in Israel's Wisconsin Plan: A Participatory Needs Assessment', Nazareth: Sawt el-Amel.
2. Sawt el-Amel: The Laborer's Voice (2005) 'Final Report'.
3. This programme is known as the Wisconsin Plan as this type of 'welfare-to-work' scheme was first implemented in the American state of Wisconsin in the mid 1990s. www.workersadvicecenter.org/Sept_05/Wisconsin.htm (last accessed September 2007).
4. Sawt el-Amel: The Laborer's Voice (2005) *op.cit.*

5. Sawt el-Amel: The Laborer's Voice (2007) 'Project Proposal: Grassroots Women's Leadership Development', Nazareth: Sawt el-Amel.
6. Sawt el-Amel: The Laborer's Voice (2006a) *op.cit.*
7. Sawt el-Amel (2007a) 'Work in Progress: Annual Report 2006', Nazareth: Sawt el-Amel, http://laborers-voice.org/files/AnnualReport_2006 per cent-5Bgeneral per cent5D.pdf (last accessed December 2007).
8. Sawt el-Amel: The Laborer's Voice (2005) *op.cit.*
9. Sawt el-Amel: The Laborer's Voice (2006a) *op.cit.*
10. Sawt el-Amel: The Laborer's Voice (2005) *op.cit.*; Sawt el-Amel: The Laborer's Voice (2006a) *op.cit.*
11. Sawt el-Amel: The Laborer's Voice (2006a) *op.cit.* Of course, this needs to be considered in light of the fact that people usually only approach Sawt el-Amel when they are in difficulties, so cannot be taken as representative.
12. A kibbutz is a collective farm.
13. Sawt el-Amel (2007a) *op.cit.*
14. Sawt el-Amel: The Laborer's Voice (2006a) *op.cit.*
15. Sawt el-Amel: The Laborer's Voice (2006a) *op.cit.*; Sawt el-Amel (2006b) 'Major Victory for Civil Society Struggle against the Wisconsin Plan', press release, 21 September 2006, Sawt el-Amel: Nazareth, http://laborers-voice.org/files/060921_Yishai.pdf (last accessed December 2007).
16. Sawt el-Amel: The Laborer's Voice (2006a) *op.cit.*
17. Sawt el-Amel: The Laborer's Voice (2007b) 'Project Proposal: *Grassroots Women's Leadership Development*', Nazareth: Sawt el-Amel.
18. Sawt el-Amel (2007a) *op.cit.* For further examples of test cases brought on behalf of women denied access to benefits for 'refusing to work', see www.laborers-voice.org.
19. Sawt el-Amel (2006b) *op.cit.* These changes also affect men and women who are within seven years of retiring, the long-term unemployed, and those with physical or mental health problems.
20. Sawt el-Amel: The Laborer's Voice (2006a) *op.cit.*
21. Sawt el-Amel: The Laborer's Voice (2005) *op.cit.*; Sawt el-Amel (2007b) *op.cit.*
22. Sawt el-Amel: The Laborer's Voice (2005) *op.cit.*
23. Interview with Marie Badarne (Head of Research and Development, Sawt el-Amel) and Wehbe Badarne (Director, Sawt el-Amel), 2007.
24. Sawt el-Amel: The Laborer's Voice (2007b) *op.cit.*
25. Sawt el-Amel: The Laborer's Voice (2005) *op.cit.*; Sawt el-Amel: The Laborer's Voice (2006a) *op.cit.*
26. Interview with Marie Badarne (Head of Research and Development, Sawt el-Amel) and Wehbe Badarne (Director, Sawt el-Amel), 2006.
27. Sawt el-Amel: The Laborer's Voice (2006a) *op.cit.*; Interview with Marie Badarne and Wehbe Badarne (2006) *op.cit.*
28. Sawt el-Amel: The Laborer's Voice (2006a) *op.cit.*
29. *Ibid.*
30. Sawt el-Amel: The Laborer's Voice (2005) *op.cit.*
31. Sawt el-Amel: The Laborer's Voice (2006a) *op.cit.*
32. *Ibid.*
33. Interview with Marie Badarne and Wehbe Badarne (2007) *op.cit.*
34. Interview with Marie Badarne and Wehbe Badarne (2006) *op.cit.*

35. *Ibid.*
36. Sawt el-Amel: The Laborer's Voice (2007b) *op.cit.*
37. Sawt el-Amel: The Laborer's Voice (2005) *op.cit.*; Interview with Marie Badarne and Wehbe Badarne (2006) *op.cit.*; Interview with Marie Badarne and Wehbe Badarne (2007) *op.cit.*
38. Sawt el-Amel: The Laborer's Voice (2006a) *op.cit.*
39. Sawt el-Amel: The Laborer's Voice (2007b) *op.cit.*
40. *Ibid.*

CHAPTER 8

Advocacy and national elections: women's political participation in Honduras

Maite Matheu

This chapter discusses Oxfam's advocacy work in Honduras on women's political rights, and women's leadership and empowerment in the political sphere. Beginning with an overview of the constraints that women face if they wish to participate in politics, the chapter then goes on to discuss Oxfam's advocacy and campaigning activities during and after the 2005 election period. These include lobbying and advocacy on political reform, campaigning to encourage people to consider voting for female candidates, and promoting women's leadership and political empowerment.

Overview: barriers to women's political participation

Honduras has been classified as the third poorest country in Latin America and the Caribbean after Haiti and Nicaragua. High levels of inequality have persisted and deepened, with income concentrated in a few hands. Eighty per cent of the population live in poverty, and absorb only 37 per cent of the gross domestic product (GDP), while the rest goes to the rich.[1] Gender inequality makes women particularly vulnerable to poverty, limiting as it does their access to employment opportunities, assets, and public services such as health care, education, and water and sanitation. As a result, women's incomes are on average only 42 per cent of men's, lower than in other Latin American countries such as Nicaragua and Bolivia.[2] The poverty faced by so many women means that they have to prioritize earning income to support themselves and their children, meaning they have little time left to think about participating in political life. In addition, lack of economic resources means that few women have the money to finance an electoral campaign.

Honduras is a strongly patriarchal society, where the church retains considerable influence in social, economic, and political life. Women are expected to devote their lives to bearing and raising children, and it is only relatively recently that most girls in Honduras have started going to school. Many older women still lack education. This places constraints on their capacity to participate in politics, as does a lack of support from family, the community, and political party members. Rural women in particular face harsh conditions, often having to walk long distances to fetch water for their families, or to accompany their children to school or to visit health centres. This means that many do not have the time, energy, or support to engage in politics.

The current political system does not address the demands of the majority of the population, in particular those of women. The system is characterized by a centralized government with a vertical power structure, and presidencialism, in which the president has ultimate power over all other state institutions.[3] The existence of a two-party system, where the two majority parties alternately gain control over Parliament (despite there being five active political parties), has been an obstacle to Parliament fulfilling its function of representing the population, and acting as an intermediary between the people and the state. Rather, the two dominant political parties have acted in the interests of the economic elites to which their leaders are linked, remaining unaccountable to the majority of the population and resistant to democratic reforms that could facilitate the promotion of gender equality and pro-poor policy. In particular, traditionally these elites have ignored and marginalized women as political subjects. This is evident in the fact that after 50 years of women's suffrage, in 2001 only 7.4 per cent of representatives in the national congress were women, and, apart from during a brief period in the early 1980s, the number of women who are mayors has never exceeded ten per cent.

'Women are discriminated [against] inside our own parties, [the men] have their own separate meetings, they have their closed groups, and they don't even invite us. Moreover, women fear participating in politics, because people start spreading lies about our behaviour, they give us nicknames, and there is ideological and sexual harassment.' (Miriam Perez, ex candidate for mayor in the municipality of Marcala)

Civil-society support to women's political leadership

In this context, Oxfam worked with Movimiento de Mujeres por la Paz 'Visitación Padilla'[4] and Centro de Estudios de la Mujer Honduras (CEM-H),[5] two feminist organizations, on a campaign aimed at changing policies and practices to increase women's political participation in the 2005 presidential, congressional, and local elections. The campaign consisted of two stages; lobbying for electoral reform, and then voter education and mobilization during the election period, accompanied by attempts to encourage candidates to adopt agendas that were supportive of women's rights, and pro-poor.

Electoral reform

The two central demands in terms of electoral reform were switching to an open preferential system for electing candidates, and the introduction of a 50 per cent quota for women candidates in both local and national elections. Political parties were also asked to develop gender-equity plans and to be more accountable to the electorate. Finally, the campaign called for a reduction in the campaign period, to make it easier for women candidates, who are likely to have less time and fewer financial resources, to stand for election.[6] One of the key strategies of the campaign was working in alliance with a coalition of civil-society organizations that supported electoral reform, leading to the coalition including the goal of equal representation of women in its agenda.

This campaign had some success. The Electoral and Political Organizations Law, which came into force in 2005, introduced an open preferential system. Under the new system, people can vote for candidates for president and for congress from different parties, whereas under the old system, voting for a presidential candidate from one party meant voting for congress members and local officials of the same party. An innovation of the system is that it includes pictures of the candidates, making it easier for people with limited literacy to vote. In addition, congress did agree to include a quota for women candidates. The efforts of congresswomen from across the political spectrum to influence the debate within congress were crucial to this; however, despite their hard work, the quota was eventually set at 30 per cent, not 50 per cent, without specifying where women candidates should be placed on electoral lists. Also, the parties interpreted the quota as a maximum ceiling.

In the primary[7] elections in 2005, only four out of 12 factions within the two main political parties complied with the quota. Those four placed women on the lower rungs of the list of candidates or as alternate members[8] of congress.[9] Rules should have been established guaranteeing compliance with the quota not only regarding the numbers of women candidates, but also the ranking of women candidates on electoral lists. This was a lesson learned by those active in the campaign: it is not enough to modify laws, because unless there is political will and a challenge to embedded cultural practices, these modifications will simply be ignored.[10] In addition, although working in alliance with other civil-society organizations and ensuring that this alliance included the goal of women's equal representation was a significant achievement, as one of the interviewees reflected, mixed organizations that did not have a women's rights focus responded to other interests. Therefore, it might have been more effective to create a separate coalition of women's rights organizations to negotiate the reforms.

Voter mobilization and lobbying candidates

Once electoral reform had been introduced, the campaign moved to educating the electorate about the new election procedures, and encouraging them to consider women candidates for congress as an electoral option, rather than simply dismissing them on the grounds that women do not make suitable political leaders. The main strategies were: raising awareness among the population about the new electoral reforms, and encouraging them to vote; and lobbying male and female candidates to include women's demands in their election manifestos.

Visitación Padilla worked intensely in 14 of the 18 departments of the country, educating women about the new election procedures, and encouraging them to consider voting for female candidates. This included stressing to voters that they now had the right to vote for presidential and congress candidates from different parties. Visitación Padilla facilitated a range of activities, such as workshops in rural areas to teach women about the new electoral system, and meetings between women candidates for congress and women from poor areas to allow the latter to present their demands.

CEM-H, for its part, lobbied candidates to adopt a progressive, women's rights agenda, and then encouraged women voters to consider supporting them. Their campaign slogan was 'mujer ya no planches', the verb 'planchar' having a double meaning in Spanish – 'to iron' or 'to make a terrible mistake'. Hence, this slogan conveyed the message to women that they should stop doing both. This campaign challenged cultural and social stereotypes about the role of women, but also invited women to vote for those congress candidates that had proposals on the issues of reproductive health, violence against women, and access to resources such as land. Linked to this, intense lobbying work was carried out among male and female candidates, to convince them to include women's demands on their agendas. This involved CEM-H visiting individual candidates from all the different political parties to raise their awareness of women's rights and poverty issues, and organizing public forums at the local level, where women articulated their concerns, and presented their demands. These demands routinely related to the provision of adequate housing and public services, and access to land. To ensure that poorer women were able to participate actively at these forums, CEM-H identified women to attend the events in advance, and provided training to boost their self-esteem and prepare them to speak in front of an audience. In addition, transport to the forums was provided.

An important feature of this work was encouraging congressional candidates and candidates for local-government positions to sign 'pacts' at local forums, declaring their commitment to women's rights and to addressing the demands identified by the women in their constituencies, particularly with regards to poverty, access to land, housing and public services, and violence against women. This was an important method of engaging male leaders in particular, who recognized that including priorities identified by poorer women in their election manifestos would translate into increased votes from women in their constituencies.

Among the campaign's achievements was prompting public discussion about women's human rights for the first time in Honduras. Also, formerly 'taboo' issues such as abortion and sexual and reproductive rights were included on the agendas of some male and female candidates. Women's increased knowledge about the political system and legislative reform are also important outcomes of this work, as was the fact that people increasingly came to recognize women candidates as an election alternative.

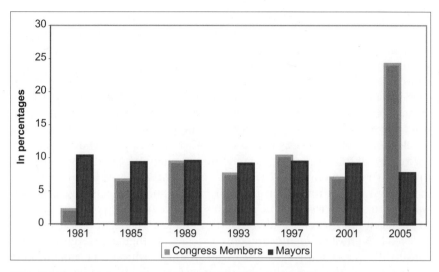

Figure 8.1 Honduras: women in national congress and in local governments
Source: Centro de Derechos de Mujeres (CDM) (2004) 'Mujeres en Cifras', Honduras;
UNDP (2006) 'Informe sobre Desarrollo Humano Honduras 2006: Hacia la expansión de la
ciudadanía'.

In November 2005, the election process closed. The most visible outcome was a significant increase in women's participation as election candidates. A total of 170 women stood for election to the national congress, of whom 31 were elected as full members and 27 as alternate members. This was a significant achievement, as it meant that women went from comprising just seven per cent (2001) of congress members, to comprising 24.2 per cent.

There was less success at the local level, where only 23 women were elected as mayors (out of 298 municipalities; or just 7.7 per cent[11]); four fewer than the number elected in 2001. It is clear that more effort should have gone into encouraging people to vote for female candidates to local government, as well as those standing for congress.

More women in congress: progress, threats, and challenges

The general elections in 2005 represented important progress for women involved in politics in Honduras. Nevertheless, this result was overshadowed by the arrival to power of women from the economic elite and conservative religious groups, who in general have no gender awareness, and are primarily concerned with the interests of their political parties. 'They were the ones who made most of the changes in the legislation, given that they had the economic resources for campaigning and also had [access to] the political networks with the two majority parties', said Suyapa Martínez of CEM-H, feminist and former candidate to congress. In contrast, many of the progressive women candidates with whom CEM-H and Visitación Padilla worked did not have sufficient financial backing to pay for campaigning, as they did not come from wealthy backgrounds, and also did not have the full backing of the political parties to which they were allied. In many cases, women candidates found themselves at the bottom of electoral lists, or not selected at all, as parties failed to implement the 30 per cent quota. Both these factors point to the need to continue to press for electoral reform, to reduce the costs of standing for election in Honduras, as well as to ensure that the 30 per cent quota is respected by all the political parties, and that momentum to increase the quota to 50 per cent is maintained. In a promising recent sign, an alliance of women in congress, women active in political parties, and women's organizations, was able to convince one of the most conservative parties to propose a reform to the Electoral Law that would raise the quota to 50 per cent.

The election of women from conservative and religious backgrounds is a threat to women's rights, given that the groups to which they are allied are promoting public policies that go against civic freedoms, and reproduce stereotypes that maintain gender inequality.[12] For instance, the Family Congress Commission, a religious bloc within congress led by a woman from the conservative Catholic organization Opus Dei, has been responsible for introducing two laws which would prohibit the introduction of sex education with a gender perspective into public schools, and stop teachers from using sex-education guides prepared by the Ministry of Education. This shows how important it is to recognize that higher numbers of women elected to political positions will not automatically lead to progressive policies that will benefit other women, or other marginalized groups. It also indicates the ongoing need to try and raise awareness of gender inequality and its impact among all electoral candidates and elected officials consistently across all the political parties, rather than just working with those who already have progressive women's rights and pro-poor agendas.

Another key challenge identified is that encouraging poorer women to participate in politics as candidates for election is difficult in a social context where most women have little experience of political processes, no access to resources, little education, and are illiterate. Activities such as lobbying parties to include poorer women on electoral lists, and providing training in public speaking and campaigning to women candidates from disadvantaged backgrounds did form part of Visitación Padilla and CEM-H's programmes, but had a limited impact. In the longer term, one change that CEM-H and others are calling for is the implementation of a preferential open electoral system at local level, similar to that which is now in place for presidential and congress elections. Suyapa Martínez argues that this would make it easier for poorer women to stand for election, as so many women are already active and well-known in their communities at the village level, and so would be more likely to be selected by political parties keen to field candidates with a high chance of winning. But even with reforms such as this, it is likely to remain difficult for poorer women to hold positions of political leadership. This is mainly due to their lack of economic and strategic resources to stand for election, both of which need to be addressed, but also because women continue to suffer discrimination and marginalization, as well as facing rigid perceptions about their role, which seek to confine them to the reproductive sphere. It will take many years of careful and systematic effort to bring about changes in attitudes, so that poor women standing for election have the support of their families, communities, and political parties.

> 'The road is long and difficult, we have to walk a long way to overcome [current attitudes to] women's role in society, their low academic level, their three-shift day, the daily struggle to survive, the church's [influence], and low self-esteem. All these are obstacles, but they can be overcome as women gain awareness and become committed and [recognize their own political value].' (Gladys Lanza, Coordinadora del Movimiento por la Paz Visitación Padilla)

Supporting progressive leadership

In the context of these challenges, Oxfam in Honduras is continuing to work with Visitación Padilla, CEM-H, and another partner organization, Centro de Derechos de Mujeres (CDM)[13] on supporting women leaders to advocate on women's rights. One aspect of this work is to facilitate links between congresswomen who have been identified as progressive, and women's rights organizations, for the exchange of ideas and information. In this regard, Oxfam partners provided support to women's rights organizations in terms of building their capacity to influence these congresswomen. These organizations have then gone on to provide training and information to congresswomen on women's rights issues, meaning that they are then in a better position to debate on bills related to women's rights within congress. As one of the interviewees commented, 'The result of this alliance with female congress members has been that no other congress in Latin America has debated so much the issue of sexual and reproductive health as in Honduras'. Although the process is far from over, precedents have been set in terms of improving the capacity of women's organizations to undertake advocacy work and in-depth analysis of the issues on which they work.

> 'The strategy of training women that have been elected and female public officials in important sectors...has been fundamental, since in a relatively short time, these women have identified with the feminist fight'. (Maritza Gallardo, Oxfam Project Co-ordinator during the campaign)

Oxfam and its partners have also worked with women who are active in political parties across the political spectrum, providing training in leadership, organization, and gender awareness. This has had a positive impact in terms of enabling these party activists to play a greater role in decision-making within their parties, and encouraging them to design and press for gender-equity plans. It has also meant that women active within political parties have supported electoral reform proposals submitted by women's organizations, encouraging their parties to adopt them.

Another strategy that is being implemented is supporting women's networks and organizations to be more effective in terms of influencing the public agenda and budget design at the local level. Some of the main activities involved are workshops for female local-government officials on women's rights and advocacy strategies, meetings with women's networks to set plans for monitoring the local pacts signed by candidates during the election, and meetings between women's networks, civil-society organizations, and members of local government. Workshops have also been held for female leaders and local officials in budget planning and social auditing[14] with a gender perspective. One positive outcome of this work has been that policies to increase women's participation have been implemented in six municipalities where Oxfam is working. As a result, female local officials have been able to participate in budget design, leading to the allocation of public resources for projects directly benefiting women at the local level.

The political empowerment of poor women

The political empowerment of poor women is also an area that has been prioritized, in recognition that earlier activities had not fully succeeded in ensuring that their needs and priorities were reflected in the agendas of the women who were actually elected to congress, and to local government. Oxfam has worked on this with two other partner organizations: the Coordinator of Rural Women of La Paz (COMUCAP)[15] and the Institute of Social Investigation and Advocacy (IISI).[16]

One important activity is work with female indigenous farmers, one of the most marginalized groups in Honduran society. In 2006, 21 indigenous women farmers active in COMUCAP took part in training at an 'Advocacy School'. These schools have been run since 2003 by IISI with support from Oxfam, and provide training to civil society and community leaders. Training is tailored to the needs of each organization, and consists of a mixture of theory and practical work. For this Advocacy School, IISI developed a training programme with activists from COMUCAP, which had a specific gender focus. Training covered:

- different kinds of leadership
- policies, laws, and institutional frameworks to promote gender equality
- processes related to the formation of public policies (setting the agenda, formulation and monitoring), with a focus on the implementation of the poverty reduction strategy paper and policies relating to access to land
- citizenship and the state

- strategies for advocacy: popular mobilization, organization, education, and working with the media

Measures were also taken to make it easier for women to participate, such as providing child-care during the course.

During the evaluation meeting, the women who had participated stated that they felt stronger, and better able to communicate their needs and interests to authorities and community organizations. They now recognized the importance of trying to influence decision-making processes that affect their lives, and had a better sense of their rights and responsibilities as citizens, and of the important contribution that they make to the economy. Increased understanding of how local- and national-level policies are formulated and implemented meant that the women now felt they were in a much better position to influence these processes.

As a result of their training, these women have designed an advocacy plan to press for more public funding for projects benefiting women, as well as contributing to the design of community-level development projects. As the mayor of Chinacla said to one leader of COMUCAP, 'you have transformed the women of Chinacla; before they didn't attend meetings and now they are the ones who speak more and advocate for women's projects'. In addition, in other districts, two women who participated in the Advocacy School are intending to run as candidates for mayor themselves.

Conclusions and recommendations

Despite advances in Honduras in developing a legal framework to promote women's participation in elected government, the gap between women's formal rights to political participation, and most women's experiences, is significant. Measures to increase the numbers of women elected have succeeded, but so far it is mainly women linked to political, economic, and religious elites who have benefited from this, leading to legislation that threatens to deny women's rights, rather than supporting them. In light of this, Oxfam and its partners have come to recognize that in addition to lobbying to increase the numbers of women elected, and lobbying for more accountable democratic systems, strategies are also required to ensure that women and men reaching power are aware of gender issues, particularly those affecting poorer women, and are prepared to work to uphold women's rights. For this purpose, it is important to continue and intensify work with women who are active in political parties or who are community or civil-society leaders, who may in the future become elected representatives and leaders, to modify their ideas and beliefs related to women's human rights, and stereotypes about gender roles.

In addition, greater attention needs to be paid to enabling poor and indigenous women to hold public positions, to ensure that policy decisions reflect the needs and interests of this group. This should include training in leadership skills and on how the political system works, to boost poorer women's confidence and knowledge, both of which are barriers to their active participation in the political sphere. It is also necessary to advocate at the government level for the implementation of public policies for gender equity, particularly those related to greater access to and control over resources. While women continue being the poorest, and the ones with the least amount of time, capacity, and experience, they will continue to be marginalized from the country's political life.

This chapter is based on both primary and secondary sources. Primary sources consist of interviews carried out with women involved in this programme, including co-ordinators of women's organizations, project managers, and women candidates who participated in the elections in 2005.

About the author

Maite Matheu is a Project Officer for Oxfam GB in Honduras.

Notes

1. Institute of Social Studies (2006) 'Evaluación de la Estrategia de Reducción de la Pobreza en América Latina, Informe de País: Honduras, 2006'.
2. UNDP (2006) 'Informe Sobre Desarrollo Humano Honduras 2006: Hacia la expansión de la ciudadanía'; Institute of Social Studies *op.cit.*
3. Civic Movement for Democracy (2003).
4. Movimiento de Mujeres por la Paz 'Visitación Padilla', or Women's Peace Movement, was created in January 1983 with the aim of raising consciousness among Hondurans regarding the US military presence in the country and the dangers of a regional war. Visitación Padilla's main aim is now to contribute to transforming the patriarchal structures that hinder women's full and equal participation in all areas of development. The organization particularly works on providing support to women who have experienced violence, and promoting women's participation as active citizens. Visitación Padilla is made up of grassroots groups of women active all over the country.
5. Centro de Estudios de la Mujer Honduras (CEM-H) was founded in 1986 as a civil not-for-profit organization without political or religious ties. The organization's mission is to contribute to the elimination of different forms of discrimination and violence against women; promote and contribute to the transformation of the economic, social, and cultural structure of the country in order to build a more inclusive society, without poverty, but with social justice and gender equality; and to enable full citizenship and the human rights of women.
6. M. Kennedy (2006) 'Situación de la Equidad de Género en Honduras', www.cemh.org.hn (last accessed November 2007).
7. In Honduras, prior to general elections, the two main political parties hold 'primary' elections to decide who will then go on to stand as candidates for president, vice president, congress, and local government in the general elections. Internal candidates represent the different political factions

within the main parties; in 2005, eight factions fielded candidates in the primary elections for the Liberal Party, and four factions fielded candidates for the National Party. All registered voters are eligible to take part. The three other parties have alternative processes to select candidates, that are not open to voters from outside the parties.

8. When a full member of congress is absent, an alternate takes his or her place. When this happens, the alternate has the same rights and responsibilities as the full member.

9. Centro de Investigación y Promoción de los Derechos Humanos (2005) 'Una mirada al proceso electoral primario 2005'.

10. M. A. Martínez (2004) 'Ponencia en el Foro Mujeres en Espacios de Toma de Decisiones'.

11. UNDP (2006) *op.cit.*

12. Centro de Derechos de Mujeres (2007) 'Memoria Foro Mujeres en Espacios de Toma de Decisiones', Tegucigalpa, Honduras, 21–23 July 2004, pp. 72–9.

13. Created in 1992, Centro de Derechos de Mujeres (CDM) is a feminist organization that promotes and defends women's rights. CDM's mission is to contribute to transforming values, attitudes, and practices that discriminate against women, in order to build a more just and equal society. CDM's principal areas of work are domestic and sexual violence, labour rights, sexual and reproductive rights, non-sexist education, and citizen participation.

14. The process of social auditing allows an organization or institution to monitor the social, economic, and environmental impact of its activities. For more information see www.socialauditnetwork.org.uk/what%202. htm (last accessed November 2007).

15. The Coordinator of Rural Women of La Paz (COMUCAP) was started in 1993 by six women who were concerned about their own living conditions, and those of other Lenca indigenous women. It now has over 250 members, and 16 local groups in four municipalities in La Paz, one of the five poorest departments (or provinces) in Honduras. COMUCAP's mission is to promote and defend the rights of its members and their families, and also to support the production and processing of organic products (principally coffee and aloe vera) for sale on the international market. COMUCAP also works on challenging violence against women.

16. The Institute of Social Investigation and Advocacy (IISI) has been active since the late 1990s. Its goal is to strengthen the advocacy skills of civil-society organizations and help them to establish a more influential relationship with the state. To this end IISI runs Advocacy Schools for community leaders and activists. 'Our emphasis is on the process of advocacy and multiplying learning. That's the key', said Salvador Segovia, IISI Facilitator. Advocacy training equips community leaders with strategies, skills, and ways of working, meaning that they are able to improve their lobby activities, their relationship with the media, their capacity to influence public opinion, and their alliances with other organizations.

CHAPTER 9

Fighting for women's rights in Chile: supporting women workers and promoting women's political participation

Michael van Gelderen

Contributor: Cecilia Millan

Despite being considered one of the most economically successful countries in Latin America, Chile is marked by high levels of social inequality. Women working in the agricultural and fish-farming sectors are particularly marginalized, and often work in unacceptable conditions, with little opportunity to challenge exploitative practices or to influence political decisions. This chapter describes Oxfam GB's strategies to increase women's leadership and participation in economic and political sectors. It looks at the impact of these strategies and presents lessons learned.

Background

Chile suffered a violent military coup in 1973 and was under the military dictatorship of General Augusto Pinochet until 1990. The transition to democracy has been slow, and many aspects of the legal, political, and economic system have been only partially reformed.

The Chilean economy is dependent on the exports of the mining, forestry, wine, fruit, and salmon industries, and the government aggressively pursues a policy of open trade relations,[1] and attracting external investment in its main export sectors and service industries. Poverty rates are relatively low, but Chile remains a very unequal society, with power concentrated in the hands of a small elite. Economic and labour rights are often seen by the economic and political elites as contradicting Chile's aim to increase economic growth and productivity, and attract and retain foreign investment.

Trade union affiliation is stagnating at low levels after having fallen for many years, and Chile has a fragmented civil society. In general, participation is strikingly low in the Chilean political system and in the design and implementation of government social and economic policies and programmes. Women in particular have traditionally found it very difficult to succeed in the political arena, dominated as it is by the interests of male elites. As a result, women's needs in particular have traditionally not been taken into account or prioritized.

Many women face a range of other problems related to gender injustices: discrimination in the workforce; labour-market segmentation that entails more precarious working conditions for women (especially in low-skilled work in the services or agro-export sectors); high levels of domestic violence; and marginalization within the political and legal systems.[2] They over-whelmingly have to bear the burden of unpaid household domestic work, yet employers do not take this into account, and fail to provide adequate measures to ease the pressure on women of this unfair double workload. The election of Michelle Bachelet as president in 2006 has, however, opened up new spaces for political participation. Her election is a powerful symbol of the possibility of change in Chile, and she is an important role model for younger women wishing to attain positions of leadership. Not only is Bach-elet a woman, she is also separated, a single mother, and suffered imprison-ment and torture during the dictatorship. Though she comes from the same political coalition that has been in power since the transition to democracy, part of her electoral appeal was that she was more distant from the tradi-tional political elite than other candidates, and promised greater concern for the issues faced by Chilean women. Her government has largely continued previous economic policy, but has expanded social spending. As a candidate, she campaigned on an explicit gender equality and justice platform, and as president she has introduced important measures to increase gender equality and justice. For instance, her government has increased child-care provision for low-income working mothers and is introducing pension reforms that will ensure a basic pension for all low-income workers (partly as a result of the awareness-raising work undertaken by Oxfam GB's partner ANAMURI, detailed below). This will benefit poor working women in particular, who were for the most part excluded from the previous pensions system. In ad-dition, her government has introduced measures to increase the protection of sexual and reproductive rights by improving access to contraception, in-cluding emergency contraception, as well as introducing measures to try and reduce high rates of domestic violence against women.

Bachelet's government is also submitting to congress a draft law that would establish a minimum quota of 30 per cent of candidates from each gender in electoral lists for both congress and the senate, in part thanks to the constant lobby work by Oxfam GB partner Humanas; and her first cabinet had an equal number of women and men ministers.

Oxfam GB's programme in Chile

Oxfam GB has been operating in Chile since the 1960s. In 2000, Oxfam GB in Chile shifted from providing institutional support to partners carrying out work at a local level to a more focused and strategic approach aimed at bringing about change through advocacy and campaigning. Promoting gender justice has been the main focus of this work, as Oxfam GB has sought to build alliances across political and ideological divides, integrate gender justice into broader agendas, and link national work with regional and global work.

Currently, Oxfam GB in Chile has a dual strategy for gender justice in the Chilean and the South American context, based on:

1. Increasing the leadership and participation of women workers with precarious employment conditions in the agriculture sector, and encouraging respect of their labour rights.
2. Increasing women's leadership and participation in politics and decision-making in Chile and in South America more widely.

The strategies complement and support each other. On the one hand, Oxfam GB is supporting some of the most marginalized women in Chile – women working as seasonal labourers in agriculture and the salmon industry – to organize and obtain better working conditions. On the other hand, it is providing support to women's organizations working to change political systems to increase the participation of women in decision-making, and to influence lawmakers and governments to increase the protection of women's rights in the workplace and beyond. The first strategy is producing valuable information about working conditions within these sectors, which is then being used in the design of draft legislation and lobbying activities undertaken in the second strategy. The latter impacts positively on all women, but in particular the most marginalized, who have most to benefit from improved working regulations and social assistance provision. It is also helping to create an improved framework to provide effective protection of women's rights, and new spaces for real participation in decision-making; both key resources that can be used by marginalized women attempting to improve their living conditions and fight gender inequality.

The programme work on labour rights and women's leadership in the economic sphere takes place in the regions in the centre and south of Chile, and in specific areas of other South American countries, where export industries producing fruit, vegetables, flowers, and fish are concentrated. The programme work on political participation and leadership is being implemented at a national and regional level, at the level of government, legal systems, and regional organizations.

Strategy 1: Upholding women's rights and promoting women's leadership in the agricultural and fish-farming sectors

Context and challenges

Recent years have seen a significant growth in the agricultural and salmon-export industries, with large numbers of women entering the workforce. Women working in the agricultural-export sectors in Chile and across South America are usually employed on an informal and seasonal basis. They often have no contracts, and are hired on a daily basis by itinerant intermediaries who work for farmers who sell to the big agro-export companies. Working conditions are frequently bad: workers receive insufficient protection against the sun and against pesticides and other chemicals used in agricultural work; they are expected to work longer hours than the legal limit in their respective countries and receive no pay for overtime; and they are not allowed sufficient breaks to eat or go to the bathroom. In addition, they have no access to adequate child-care, and have no, or limited access to state health care and pensions systems. The working conditions of women are usually worse than those of men in the same line of work, and women face segmentation into more mechanical and low-paid activities. Women agricultural workers often come from rural areas, and some have to leave their homes for several weeks or months to go and work during the season for a particular fruit or vegetable, or travel from place to place in the agricultural areas looking for work. There is little public awareness of the economic contribution these women make to the success of these high-profile industries, or of the conditions in which they have to work.

In Chile, these informal workers have no trade unions. This is because Chilean legislation does not allow them to form trade unions (since they do not work for one employer), and any attempt at organizing themselves or making demands for improved working conditions leads to blacklisting by the intermediaries, and to the loss of work. Moreover, traditional trade unions and workers' organizations have usually ignored the situation of seasonal women workers, because the temporary, seasonal, and informal nature of the work makes it difficult to organize these workers. The one exception is the salmon sector, where there are trade unions operating along more traditional lines.

In response to this, in Chile many small groups of women agricultural workers and small-scale producers have emerged, which have now come under a national network called Asociación Nacional de Mujeres Rurales e Indígenas (National Association of Rural and Indigenous Women), or ANAMURI.

Programme activities and impact

Oxfam GB has supported specific activities carried out by the ANAMURI network to organize, lobby, raise funds, receive technical assistance through NGO partners, build alliances with other civil-society organizations, and contact and build alliances with women agricultural workers in other countries. In Chile, these activities have been successful. The women active in the ANAMURI network have managed to raise public and political awareness of their existence and precarious working conditions, gathering and making public information obtained through their network of members. They have managed to place their demands on the public agenda and negotiate with the ministries of health, labour, agriculture, and women, all of which now recognize their organization as a valid interlocutor.[3] For instance, members of ANAMURI played a key role in highlighting the large number of workers not covered by the current pensions system. The awareness they raised and the technical input they provided to the Pensions Reform Commission in 2006 has helped to shape the new pensions law which is currently going through congress, that establishes a minimum pension for poor Chileans,[4] regardless of whether or not they have managed to save sufficient funds in their individual pension account. This will mean that many low-income, subcontracted women workers will have access to basic pensions for the first time, including those working in agriculture, commerce, and service industries. Similarly, ANAMURI have raised awareness of the negative impact of subcontracted labour relations on working conditions, and thanks in part to their lobbying, this practice is now more regulated. Companies that use subcontracted labour now have legal obligations towards these workers (in terms of health and safety, and social-security contributions), even if no direct contractual relationship exists. Members of ANAMURI have also participated in provincial, national, regional, and international networks and discussions.

In other countries (Ecuador, Bolivia, Colombia, Peru) it has been more difficult to form as wide or successful a network of women seasonal agricultural workers as in Chile. However, there are some indications that women seasonal agricultural workers are beginning to organize. In Peru, for instance, the Aurora Vivar organization has been trying to co-ordinate a network similar to that of ANAMURI in Chile.

Oxfam GB has also encouraged and supported labour and environmental 'observatories'. These bring together different workers' organizations, labour-rights NGOs, and environmental NGOs in a particular geographical area to analyse labour conditions and the environmental impact of a particular industry (in this case, fruit and salmon export industries), and to raise awareness of these through the media and other communications activities. Observatories also offer opportunities for lobbying and advocacy in congress and special government commissions to improve labour conditions and reduce the environmental impact of these industries, and for dialogue between workers, local communities, and provincial and local authorities and businesses. Lobbying, awareness raising, and dialogue have centred around such issues as: the substandard application of safety regulations, leading to above-average rates of accident and death, especially among subcontracted workers; forcing workers to work more than the legal maximum number of working hours per day; continuing operations when port authorities have ordered that they should cease (in the case of the salmon industry); harassment and discrimination against women, especially pregnant women and working mothers; failure to provide child-care facilities, when required by law; and anti-trade union practices. Oxfam GB assisted in the organization of these observatories, and has helped to integrate a gender perspective, and to ensure that the working conditions of women workers in particular are considered. Oxfam GB has also helped to manage the media and communications strategy for the observatories, as well as provide support with campaigns: these are usually weak areas for organizations that work in this context.

Oxfam GB is also supporting the development of a regional (Andean) network of agro-export workers' organizations to promote and defend workers' labour rights in this sector in the region. It has also supported women's organizations that have organized public tribunals in Chile and several other South American countries to highlight gross abuses of economic, social, and cultural rights. These public tribunals have generated media attention and increased public awareness, and have also led to cases being brought to trial in several countries, with some success. These have included the improved protection of women agricultural workers from pesticides in the agro-export industry in Chile.

Lessons learned

In contexts such as those of the agro-export industries in Chile, where trade unions are weak or non-existent, or otherwise are not providing adequate support to the increasing number of women workers, it is important for organizations committed to women's rights in development to support new and alternative forms of workers' organizations, including women workers' organizations such as ANAMURI. Like trade unions, these worker organizations can often be traditional in their hierarchical structure. Oxfam GB has encouraged more participatory approaches to leadership through supporting annual congresses, for instance. However, in this context, the scope for supporting changes in ways of working is determined by the nature of Oxfam GB's support of ANAMURI, which is limited to supporting specific activities and facilitating links with other organizations.

In the salmon industry, work is less seasonal in nature, making it easier for formal trade unions and labour-rights NGOs to act on behalf of workers. Oxfam GB has sought to promote the leadership and participation of women in these mixed workers' organizations and trade unions through the labour and environmental observatory of Chiloé island, but this has been a challenge. For example, in December 2006 at the Chiloé observatory, Oxfam GB supported the election of a young woman worker as the head of a large confederation of trade unions; by June 2007, she had resigned, due to overwork and lack of support. This indicates how much support and ongoing training is needed by women elected to leadership positions in such male-dominated environments, in order to carry out their work. As a result, Oxfam GB is providing support and training to women workers in the salmon industry in order to promote their leadership skills and strengthen the incorporation of a gender perspective in their work, to enable them to identify and make visible the specific needs and rights of women workers. In addition, Oxfam GB recognizes that work needs to be done with male leaders within the trade unions, to ensure that they are ready to work with their female counterparts so that the latter are able to participate fully in collective negotiations and other deci-sion-making processes.

Working at the local and regional level through observatories has allowed alliances between different organizations around specific issues (labour condi-tions, environmental impact) in specific industries. The observatories have had an impact on specific processes at the local and provincial level (e.g. spe-cific collective negotiation processes), and they have enabled dialogue forums with local authorities and the private sector, where women workers have also participated. Moreover, they have managed to gain media coverage and place the issues on the public agenda. However, the work of the observatories has not yet led to broad, sustainable improvements in the working conditions of workers in the agricultural export sectors, or to respect for labour legislation. In addition, there have been difficulties in maintaining functional working relationships between the different observatory partners.

In response to this, a campaign will be developed on working conditions in the salmon industry in 2008–2009 that will test the effectiveness of the observatory platform at a national level.

Strategy 2: Increasing women's leadership and participation in politics and decision-making in Chile and South America

Context and challenges

Traditionally, Chile's political and governance systems are characterized by limited citizen participation. Political decisions are often taken with elite in-terests in mind, and those social policies aimed at poor and/or excluded sec-tors of the population are usually neither designed nor implemented with their participation. The military dictatorship left an electoral and representa-tive system that artificially induces and perpetuates the existence of two broad coalitions. On one side, there is the politically broad socialist/Christian/liberal democrat governing coalition of several political parties that has been in pow-er for 17 years, since the end of the dictatorship. This coalition is characterized by the lack of a unified political project, and very diverse positions among the different factions. They have maintained the neo-liberal economic policies established during the dictatorship years, but have added measures to serve as social safety nets. This has succeeded in reducing poverty, but has made no significant progress in tackling the high level of inequality. On the other side, the right-wing coalition, the political heir of the dictatorship, is formed of two parties. One of these has more grassroots support, and both have strong sup-port among the conservative economic and political elite. Under the electoral system inherited from the Pinochet dictatorship, the opposition coalition is over-represented in both congress and the senate. Fifteen per cent of repre-sentatives in the lower chamber of congress are women, while in the upper chamber the figure is just five per cent.

Surveys of women in Chile carried out in 2006 and 2007 and supported by Oxfam GB indicated a low level of political engagement among women. They showed that 52 per cent of women surveyed did not identify with any of the political parties, while 63 per cent showed no interest in obtaining information on the work of their representative in congress. Of the 37 per cent of women who declared an interest in the work of their representative, around a quarter (23 per cent) did try and engage with their representative in some way or another. The women surveyed did have clear ideas about the urgent need to reform certain legislation, such as that relating to child support from absent fathers, the lack of child-care facilities for working parents, and the need to introduce a mechanism that would guarantee equal access for women and men to elected positions – issues that have been taken up by the Bachelet government and were part of her electoral platform. Over half of the women surveyed did not feel that either coalition sufficiently promotes their interests as women, though the governing coalition obtains better marks, and Michelle Bachelet obtains good marks for her concern for women's issues.[5] That said, over 80 per cent of those surveyed indicated that the election of Michelle Bachelet had not increased their interest in politics, though 64 per cent do expect that at the end of her presidency, their rights would be better protected.

The surveys also asked women to indicate what they thought were the main obstacles women faced in terms of occupying leadership positions. In the 2007 survey, 70 per cent of women respondents identified the principal difficulty facing women decision-makers as a lack of respect for their decisions, due to stereotypical assumptions that men should be the ones to make decisions. The previous year, women surveyed had identified the principal difficulties as having to prove themselves more than men (36 per cent), having more household obligations (29 per cent), and facing discrimination in political parties (20 per cent). Over 80 per cent of the women surveyed thought that there should be laws establishing parity between the number of men and women in decision-making positions in congress, the senate, the judiciary, ministries, provincial governors, the army, and public administrators.[6]

Some of the specific challenges that Oxfam GB faces in its work in this area are the lack of communication between women's organizations and other civil-society organizations, and the low overall priority (despite Michelle Bachelet's leadership) given by the government, the private sector, and mainstream civil society to issues regarded by women as a priority.

Programme activities and impact

Oxfam GB initiated the creation of, and provides ongoing support to, a coalition of organizations in Chile, including feminist organizations, academics, and governance NGOs, through a parliamentary observatory. This monitors the work of both congress and the senate, and lobbies to improve draft laws and encourage their approval so as to have a direct, positive impact on women's participation and the protection of their rights, across all levels of society.

The observatory has worked on a number of draft laws, including one which aims to establish minimum quotas for both genders in electoral lists (now under consideration in congress), another that establishes penalties for discriminatory conduct, and a draft law that would enable Chile to ratify the Rome Treaty of the International Criminal Court.[7] Other draft laws are related to making government in Chile more transparent and accountable, and the establishment of a human-rights institute.

The parliamentary observatory has been successful as one of the first unified civil-society initiatives to scrutinize the work of congress and the senate, and raise awareness of the closed and non-transparent manner in which they work. It has also succeeded in raising awareness of the low priority that is given to draft laws that impact on women's rights and political participation, by lawmakers and the government. The observatory platform has been successful in bringing together a variety of actors and organizations working on governance and women's rights and political participation, and in increasing the importance of women's political participation on the civil-society agenda. Finally, it has also lobbied to improve draft laws and accelerate or increase the probability of these draft laws being approved.

Oxfam GB has also supported a range of organizations in the region with work at national and regional levels aiming to increase women's political participation. One such example is supporting several organizations to survey women on their perceptions of the political systems and the level of discrimination in their respective countries (Argentina, Bolivia, Chile, Ecuador), then to carry out a regional seminar to compare results. The results of these surveys have helped raise awareness across the region of the opinions of women and their exclusion from politics and decision-making. They have been used by women's organizations to lobby for reforms to political systems to ensure or encourage the greater participation of women, as well as specific measures to combat discrimination and violence against women. They have also helped women's rights organizations to devise strategic plans to follow up on the results of the surveys and carry out advocacy towards improving respect for the economic, social, and cultural rights of women in individual countries and in the region.

Oxfam GB in Chile has provided key support to an alliance of NGOs operating at the regional level to lobby for an increase in the participation of women with a progressive gender perspective in regional organizations, such as the Organization of American States (OAS), MERCOSUR,[8] and the Inter-American Court of Human Rights and the Inter-American Commission on Human Rights. This included lobbying OAS regarding the appointment of new judges to the Inter-American Court of Human Rights, raising awareness of the need for judges to have an understanding of the specific rights of women. And Oxfam GB has also supported regional women's organizations to lobby regional inter-governmental institutions on key regional issues facing specific groups of women, such as women migrant workers, and women paid domestic workers (many of whom are migrant workers), in the region.

Lessons learned

The main strengths of the parliamentary observatory are that it has brought together a politically diverse range of organizations, it has managed to raise the importance of women's rights on the agendas of organizations that do not have a gender perspective in their work (e.g. NGOs working on governance issues), and it has carried out important advocacy and lobby work towards specific draft laws in Parliament. However, at times it has been difficult for those involved in the observatory to maintain interest in sharing a common platform, rather than pursuing individual institutional interests. The observatory has been successful in lobbying for specific draft laws (e.g. gender quotas in electoral lists), and has had partial success in getting media coverage and raising public interest. It has also succeeded, both through its activities as well as through its support for legal changes to increase transparency and women's participation in politics, in opening up new spaces for participation, that in turn can be used to push for improvements in the protection of women's rights (for instance, work on labour rights and social protection for low-income women workers). The limited success in raising public interest is a feature of lobby and advocacy work in a closed political system: the aim of the observatory is that with increased transparency and formal and informal mechanisms for participation, there will be increased interest from the public in general, and women in particular, in the work of Parliament that the observatory monitors.

The other regional work, including the surveys and regional lobbying work, has been successful in what it aims to do: raise awareness among governments and regional organizations, lobby for legal and administrative measures that facilitate an increase in women's participation, and as such encourage, indirectly, changes in the negative attitudes of both men and women towards women's political participation and leadership. This regional work has also been successful in building stronger alliances between organizations in different countries in the region.

Key learning points

The two strategies outlined above support each other. An example is the work on labour rights that highlighted the situation of women workers in the seasonal agricultural export industries, where information obtained from women workers about their working conditions was used to inform the lobbying strategy for work on draft laws that impact on labour rights (e.g. pension reform). Awareness-raising about the indiscriminate use of pesticides without adequate safety provisions led to tougher regulations to protect workers (mostly women). Similarly, the work on labour rights in the salmon industry has become a political issue. Workers' representatives have gone to Parliament to participate in a designated commission on the social and environmental impact of the industry (where women worker leaders participated), in part enabled by the leadership skills gained through participation in the observatory and associated training activities. There is the potential for increasing this sort of overlap in the future, for instance ensuring that political and lobbying work at provincial or local levels is informed by the local work on labour rights undertaken by the labour observatories. Another strategy will be to encourage the participation of marginalized women workers in political debates on laws that affect them, at a regional level.

One of the key learning points that Oxfam GB in Chile has drawn from its work on women's participation and leadership is that different strategies are necessary to obtain concrete improvements in the lives of women. Work on improving labour conditions has a direct positive impact on the lives of some of the most marginalized women in South America. But to have sustainable improvement in respect for women's rights, political systems and cultures have to be changed to enable the increased participation of women. Monitoring and lobbying work by women's organizations and alliances is a key part of that effort. On the other hand, lobbying and political work is more legitimate if it is based on the needs of poor and excluded women, as identified by those women themselves. As such, these strategies complement each other to achieve their common objective.

In addition, Oxfam GB's work in Chile has shown that work at the national and regional levels is mutually reinforcing, providing legitimacy to both, and a stronger platform from which to implement advocacy work. Finally, creating alliances between non-traditional allies (including women's organizations and other civil-society organizations) is key to obtaining positive political changes for women's participation and the protection of their rights in a fragmented environment, although these alliances are fragile and effort is required to maintain them.

About the author

Michael van Gelderen wrote this chapter while working as an Advocacy Officer for Oxfam GB in Chile.

Notes

1. Chile has signed the highest number of free-trade agreements of any country in the world.
2. In surveys undertaken by Oxfam GB partner Humanas in 2006 and 2007, the vast majority (88 per cent) of the women surveyed considered that women are discriminated against in Chile, and consider that discrimination is particularly prevalent in the context of work, sexuality, access to justice, politics, the media, and family life; over 60 per cent of all the women surveyed said that they suffered in their daily life as a result of such discrimination. The vast majority (95 per cent) of women surveyed indicated that they felt that violence against women by their partners is

frequent or very frequent in Chile, and 64 per cent identified violence against women as an extension of Chile's macho society.

3. In Chile, ANAMURI members have participated in the following government-organized institutions: the Agriculture Ministry's Agricultural Export Council and Agricultural Area Council, the Health Ministry's Dialogue Committee on Social Determinants of Health, the Labour Ministry's Public–Private Council, and the Women's Ministry's Rural Women National Roundtable.

4. Pensions are means-tested and subject to residency requirements. The minimum pension will be low (around half of the minimum wage) but nonetheless very significant for those who had no access to a pension before this reform.

5. In the same surveys, 63 per cent of women agreed that Bachelet has a strong or very strong concern for the problems faced by women. Women surveyed also gave her good marks for taking concrete measures to improve access to contraception methods (76 per cent) and to promote the equal participation of men and women in positions of power (72 per cent); and medium marks in terms of promoting the equal distribution of household responsibilities between men and women (55 per cent), and equal salaries between men and women (54 per cent).

6. The recent draft law on gender quotas in electoral lists should partly address this, if it is approved by Parliament.

7. This is the first international legal instrument that considers sexual violence and gender violence as crimes against humanity. This has specific relevance in Chile given the human-rights abuses, including sexual violence and torture, that occurred during the dictatorship.

8. MERCOSUR, or *Mercado Común del Sur* is a regional market integration body formed in 1985. Current members are Argentina, Uruguay, Paraguay, and Brazil. Venezuela is in the process of joining. Bolivia, Chile, Colombia, Ecuador, and Peru are 'associated states', and Mexico and Nicaragua have observer status.

CHAPTER 10
Useful resources

Joanna Hoare

Contributor: Kate Agha

Toolkits and guides

BRIDGE Cutting Edge Pack: Gender and Participation (2001)

Supriya Akerkar, Emma Bell, and Paola Brambilla

BRIDGE, Institute of Development Studies, University of Sussex, Brighton BN1 9RE, UK. Tel: +44 (0)1273 606261, Fax: +44 (0)1273 621202/691647, Website: www.bridge.ids.ac.uk
Available online at:
www.bridge.ids.ac.uk/reports_gend_CEP.html#Participation

This pack consists of an overview report and an accompanying list of useful resources. The report looks at convergences between approaches to gender and to participation, how these have been played out, and how they have been or could be constructively integrated into development projects, programmes, policies, and institutions. Successful experiences and practices are identified. Examples of failure, and mistakes to avoid, are also described.

Called to speak: six strategies that encourage women's political activism. Lessons from interfaith community organizing (2006)

Amy Caizza

Available online at: www.iwpr.org/pdf/I916.pdf

I knew I could do this work: seven strategies that promote women's activism and leadership in unions (2007)

Amy Caizza

Institute for Women's Policy Research (IWPR), 1707 L Street NW, Suite 750, Washington, DC 20036, USA. Tel: +1 (202) 785 5100, Fax: +1 (202) 833-4362, Website: www.iwpr.org
Available online at: www.iwpr.org/pdf/I917.pdf

These two reports provide ideas on how to encourage and support women's active participation and leadership in two areas where women have traditionally seldom held leadership positions: religious groups and trade unions. Both reports describe successful strategies to promote women's leadership in these spheres, backed up with case-study examples from successful programmes. While both reports have a strong US focus, they are likely to be of use to those working in these areas elsewhere.

Empowering Young Women to Lead Change: a Training Manual (2006)

World YWCA (16, Ancienne Route, CH-1218 Grand-Saconnex, Geneva, Switzerland. Tel: +41 22 929 6040, Fax: +41 22 929 6044, Email: worldoffice@ worldywca.org, Website: www.worldywca.org) and United Nations Population Fund (220 East 42nd St. New York, NY 10017 USA. Tel: +1 212 297 5000, Website: www.unfpa.org)
Available online in English, French, and Spanish at: www.unfpa.org/publications/detail.cfm?ID=304

This resource manual is designed to enable young women to prepare and facilitate training on different issues that are important to them. A joint publication of the World YWCA and UNFPA, the manual was developed by young women and contains modules on young women's leadership, economic justice, HIV and AIDS, human rights, peace, self esteem and body image, sexual and reproductive health, and violence against women. Trainings and workshops can be designed using the entire manual or pulling out modules of interest for shorter sessions.

Femmes Leaders pour un Developpement Local Durable et Equitable (Women Leaders for a Local, Sustainable, and Equal Development)

Bureau de la Coopération Suisse au Niger, B.P. 728, Niamey, République du Niger. Tel: +227 73 3916, Fax: +227 73 3313, Email: niamey@sdc.net, Website: www.ddc-niger.ch.
Available in French at: http://162.23.39.120/dezaweb/ressources/resource_fr_24870.pdf

This document aims to support the identification of women leaders and the process of leadership building. The first part looks at why women's leadership is important and includes an analysis of gender relations in Niger and of the role of women leaders in local communities. The second part looks at how to identify women leaders in their communities, including what qualities to look for, the constraints they may face, and strategies that can be used. The third part describes how to support women leaders to build their capacity. It includes strategies to help women develop their leadership skills, both at the personal and political level, as well as general actions to promote women's leadership, including how to fight prejudices and enhance women's mobility.

GET Ahead for Women in Enterprise: Training Package and Resource Kit (2006)

Susanne Bauer, Gerry Finnegan, and Nelien Haspels

International Labour Organization (ILO), Regional Office for Asia and the Pacific, 11th Floor, United Nations Building, Rajdamnern Nok Avenue, P.O. Box 2-349, Bangkok 10200, Thailand. Tel: +662 288 1234, Fax: +662 288 1735, Email: bangkok@ilo.org
Available online at: www.ilo.org/public/english/region/asro/bangkok/library/pub4c.htm

This training package is designed to promote enterprise development among women in poverty who want to start or are already engaged in small-scale business, in order to facilitate women's economic and social empowerment. It consists of a series of participatory and action-orientated training modules, all with a strong gender perspective. The pack was field-tested in Thailand, Lao PDR, and Cambodia, and brings together sources and ideas for exercises that have proved to be effective and appropriate for low-income women with little formal education, as well as for top managers in the public and in the private sector.

Leading to Choices: a leadership training handbook for women (2001)

Mahnaz Afkhami, Ann Eisenberg, and Haleh Vaziri

The Women's Learning Partnership for Rights, Development, and Peace (WLP), 4343 Montgomery Avenue, Suite 201, Bethesda, MD 20814, USA. Tel: +1 301 654 2774, Fax: +1 301 654 2775, Email: wlp@learningpartnership.org, Website: www.learningpartnership.org
Available online at: www.learningpartnership.org/docs/engltcmanual.pdf

This manual has been developed to train diverse groups of women and girls, at all levels, in the practice of inclusive, participatory, and horizontal leadership. All the activities are interactive, and have been developed in co-operation with women's organizations from a range of different countries. The manual is also available to download in Maghreby-Arabic, Shamy-Arabic, Assamese, French, Hausa, Malay, Meiteilon, Persian, Portuguese, Russian, Shona, Spanish, Swahili, Turkish, and Uzbek.

Women in Parliament: Beyond Numbers (2002)

Edited by Azza Karam

International Institute for Democracy and Electoral Assistance (International IDEA), Strömsborg, SE-103 34 Stockholm, Sweden. Tel: +46 8 698 37 99, Fax: +46 8 20 24 22, Email: info@idea.int, Website: www.idea.int
Available online at: www.idea.int/publications/wip/index.cfm

Written by parliamentarians and researchers, 'Women in Parliament: Beyond Numbers' examines the obstacles women face in getting into Parliament, how to overcome such barriers, and ways in which women can make a greater impact once they enter Parliament. It examines such topics as quotas and electoral systems and includes case studies from Costa Rica, Egypt, India, Jordan, Lebanon, Norway, Russia, and South Africa.

Women Parliamentarians Making a Difference in Politics: Worldwide Experiences and Practices (2007)

UNIFEM Afghanistan, UNDP Compound, Opp Turkish Embassy, Shar-e-Naw Kabul, Afghanistan. Tel: +93 70 28 24 46, Fax: +873 761 660 769, Email: registry.unifem.af@unifem.org, Website: http://afghanistan.unifem.org
Available online in English and Dari at: http://afghanistan.unifem.org/media/pub/index.html#toolkit2

This report provides an assessment of women active in parliaments around the world, the obstacles that they face in getting elected and in carrying out their duties, and how women parliamentarians can make a positive difference in the lives of the people that they represent. In addition to country case studies, the report includes explanations of different formal and informal mechanisms to support women in Parliament, such as mentoring schemes and building networks. Although this report was prepared for use in Afghanistan, it will be of use for others working on these issues in other parts of the world.

Organizations and networks

Association for Women's Rights in Development (AWID) – Young Feminist Activist Program

Website: www.awid.org, Email: contact@awid.org

AWID's Young Feminist Activist Program grew out of an earlier project, the Young Women's Leadership Program. The programme aims to motivate, enable, and support young women to be activists for social change through creating provocative opportunities for engagement, innovative research projects, and capacity-building activities. Links are available to a wide range of resources, including 'Act Now! A Resource Guide for Young Women on HIV/AIDS' (2002), published in association with UNIFEM (available online at: www.unifem.org/attachments/products/ActNow_eng.pdf). This booklet is targeted at young women who are leaders in their communities, and explores the ways in which young people can participate in addressing gender and youth issues in HIV and AIDS programmes. Another paper, 'Making waves: how young women can (and do) transform organizations and movements' (www.awid.org/publications/OccasionalPapers/spotlight5_en.pdf), highlights the contributions that young women are making to women's movements, and suggests strategies to overcome the obstacles that they continue to face in attaining positions of leadership within those movements.

Center for Women's Global Leadership (CWGL)

www.cwgl.rutgers.edu

Founded in 1989, the Center for Women's Global Leadership works to develop and facilitate women's leadership for women's human rights and social justice worldwide. In addition to an extensive international policy and advocacy programme, the centre facilitates leadership development and women's human-rights education workshops. The website includes links to CWGL's extensive backlist of publications, and to other resources on women's human rights.

FEMNET – the African Women's Development and Communications Network

Off Westlands Road, P. O. Box 54562, 00200 Nairobi, Kenya. Tel: +254 20 3741301/20, Fax: +254 20 3742927, Email: admin@femnet.or.ke, Website: www.femnet.or.ke

FEMNET exists to facilitate and co-ordinate the sharing of experiences, ideas, information, and strategies for human-rights promotion among African women's organizations, with the ultimate aim of advancing African women's collective leadership for equality, peace, and sustainable development. Programme work focuses on advocacy, communications, and capacity-building around gender mainstreaming. The website provides links to publications on a range of issues relating to women's rights, as well as access to an online discussion board.

I Know Politics: International Knowledge Network of Women in Politics

www.iknowpolitics.org

This 'online workspace' is targeted at women active in politics at every level, as well as other practitioners interested in advancing women's leadership in the political sphere. In addition to an active online discussion forum where members can share experience and information, the site provides links to a wide range of resources, other organizations working to promote women's leadership, and relevant news articles.

Inter-Parliamentary Union

5, chemin du Pommier, Case postale 330, CH-1218 Le Grand-Saconnex/Geneva, Switzerland. Tel: +41 22 919 41 50, Fax: +41 22 919 41 60, Email: postbox@mail.ipu.org, Website: www.ipu.org

The Inter-Parliamentary Union promotes discussion and co-operation between elected parliaments in different countries. The IPU website provides access to two very useful databases: Women in National Parliaments, which gives extensive information about the numbers of women in Parliament throughout the world; and the Women in Politics Bibliographic Database, which lists books and articles dealing with women in politics.

onlinewomeninpolitics.org – Asia Pacific Online Network of Women in Politics, Governance and Transformative Leadership

www.onlinewomeninpolitics.org

Established in 1999, onlinewomeninpolitics.org provides a means for Asia-Pacific women active in politics to network and exchange information. The site has links to useful statistics on women's representation in political structures, as well as to publications and other organizations active in this sphere. onlinewomeninpolitics.org also distributes a regular email newsletter, with a round-up of news stories on women and politics from around the world.

United Nations Development Fund for Women – UNIFEM

United Nations Headquarters, 304 East 45th Street, 15th Floor, New York, NY 10017, United States. Tel: +1 212 906 6400, Fax: +1 212 906 6705, Website: www.unifem.org

Encouraging women's political participation and engagement in peacebuilding and reconstruction processes is an important aspect of UNIFEM's work, on the basis that such participation and engagement are fundamental prerequisites for gender equality and genuine democracy. Details of the agency's work on governance, peace, and security, as well as links to useful resources, can be found at www.unifem.org/gender_issues/governance_peace_security/. In addition, UNIFEM hosts a web portal – www.womenwarpeace.org – dedicated to providing information and resources on women's participation in peacebuilding and post-conflict reconstruction.

Women's Environment and Development Organization (WEDO)

355 Lexington Ave., 3rd Floor, New York, NY 10017, USA. Tel: +1 212 973 0325, Fax: +1 212 973 0335, Website: www.wedo.org

The Women's Environment and Development Organization advocates for gender equality in global policy, seeking to empower women as decision makers to achieve economic, social, and gender justice. The 50/50 Campaign aims to increase women's participation and representation in governments throughout the world. A range of useful resources can be accessed from the website, including the 50/50 Campaign Kit (www.wedo.org/campaigns.aspx?mode=5050campaignkit).

Women's Learning Partnership for Rights, Development, and Peace (WLP)

4343 Montgomery Avenue, Suite 201, Bethesda, MD 20814, USA. Tel: +1 301 654 2774, Fax: +1 301 654 2775, Email: wlp@learningpartnership.org, Website: www.learningpartnership.org

The Women's Learning Partnership works with partner organizations to promote women's leadership and empowerment, particularly in Muslim-majority countries. Its primary objectives are to increase the number of women taking on leadership and decision-making roles at family, community, and national levels, and to improve the effectiveness of feminist movements in Muslim-majority societies and globally by strengthening the capacity of partner organizations. In addition to leadership and campaigning activities, the partnership also offers leadership training. The website has an extensive resources section, as well as links to WLP's publications.

Useful background reports and papers

Beyond Victimhood: Women's Peacebuilding in Sudan, Congo and Uganda (2006)

Africa Report N°112, International Crisis Group, 149 Avenue Louise, Level 24, B-1050 Brussels, Belgium. Tel: +32 2 502 90 38, Fax: +32 2 502 50 38, Website: www.crisisgroup.org
Available online at: www.crisisgroup.org/home/index.cfm?id=4185&l=1

This report argues that for the process of peacebuilding to succeed in Sudan, Congo, and Uganda, women must be involved. National governments and the international community must do more to support women leaders and activist groups who are already working towards peace, on the grounds that women's peace movements can affect large sectors of the population and be a powerful force for reducing violence and building democratic and participatory public institutions, particularly in the post-conflict period.

Conversations with Women on Leadership and Social Transformation (2004)

Srilatha Batliwala and Aruna Rao

Gender at Work, P.O. Box 112 Glen Echo, MD 20817, USA. Website: www.genderatwork.org
Available online at: www.genderatwork.org/resources.php

Conversations with 18 women leaders from both the global South and the North present a wide range of perspectives on leadership, and women's practice of leadership for social change. While recognizing that the concepts of 'women's interests' and 'women's leadership' need always to be contextualized and broken down according to local understandings and priorities, this report suggests that women's leadership is an important element in advancing equity and social justice for all.

Equal participation of women and men in decision-making processes, with particular emphasis on political participation and leadership (2005)

Expert Group Meeting, Addis Ababa, Ethiopia, 24 to 27 October 2005. Organized by the United Nations Department of Economic and Social Affairs (DESA) Division for the Advancement of Women (DAW)
Available online at: www.un.org/womenwatch/daw/egm/eql-men/documents_preview.html

This website gives access to papers presented at the Expert Group Meeting in 2005. These papers cover a range of topics related to women's political participation and leadership, including articles on the effectiveness of quotas, women's policy machineries, political parties, and women in local government. Examples are taken from different countries, including Moldova, Costa Rica, Nigeria, and India.

Gender, Governance and Democracy: Women in Politics (2005)

ISIS Monograph Series 2005, Issue 1, Vol. 1, Isis International – Manila, 3 Marunong Street, Brgy. Central, Quezon City, Philippines. Tel: +63 2 9281956, Fax: +63 2 9241065, Website: www.isiswomen.org.

This monograph consists of two articles on women in politics. The first – 'Strategies to Enhance Women's Political Representation in Different Electoral Systems' (by Drude Dahlerup) – discusses the use of quotas to increase the number of women in political institutions, concluding that introducing quotas is an important strategy for women's political justice and empowerment under the 'right circumstances'. The second article – 'Women in Politics and Governance: Complex Challenges from Globalisation' (by Josefa 'Gigi' Francisco) – outlines the specific complexities facing women who choose to engage with the state in Asia, and argues that women's movements in the region should address more resolutely the inter-linking of economic justice and gender justice issues within alternative political spaces.

Globalization and Democratic Governance: A Gender Perspective (2002)

Noeleen Heyzer

Paper given at the Fourth Global Forum on Reinventing Government – Citizens, Businesses, and Governments: Partnerships for Development and Democracy, 11–13 December 2002, Marrakech, Morocco.
Available online at: http://unpan1.un.org/intradoc/groups/public/documents/UN/UNPAN006228.pdf

In this essay, then Executive Director of UNIFEM Noeleen Heyzer discusses the negative impacts that economic globalization is having on poor women, as well as the potential opportunities that it presents to them. Heyzer emphasizes the links between gender inequality and poverty, outlining the importance of investing in women's skills and knowledge in order to allow them to benefit from emerging employment and earning opportunities in the globalizing economy. She concludes by stressing the importance of women's economic leadership, highlighting how women leaders are already shaping the way that markets operate, bringing together ideas on gender justice and economic justice.

WomenLead in Peace and Stability (2007)

Center for Development and Population Activities, 1133 21st Street, NW Suite 800, Washington, DC 20036, USA. Tel. +1 202 667 1142, Fax +1 202 332 4496, Website: www.cedpa.org
Available online at: www.cedpa.org/content/publication/detail/1718

This report brings together testimonies from 15 women leaders from Sudan, Sierra Leone, Uganda, Côte d'Ivoire, the Solomon Islands, Kenya, the Philippines, and Nigeria. All have been active in mediating conflict, caring for refugees, restoring communities in post-conflict settings, and building more responsive governments. In addition to helping to bring about peace and stability in their communities, these women leaders are also helping to challenge and change mindsets regarding women's roles in society, and the valuable knowledge, perspectives, and experience that they can bring to leadership positions.

About the author

Joanna Hoare wrote this chapter while working for Oxfam GB. She now works as a freelance editor and writer on gender and development issues.

CHAPTER 11
Concluding update

Joanna Hoare

Contributors: Menh Navy, Marie-Olivia Badarne, Sue Smith,
Mary Wandia, Muhamned Bizimana, Kristie van Wetering,
Maite Matheu, Gaynor Tanyang, Jing Pura, Rosa Wilson
Garwood, Fiona Gell, Ines Smyth, John Cropper, Jo Rowlands,
Mary Wandia, and Katie Allan

The case studies included in this book document the programme and advocacy work of Oxfam's partners on strengthening women's participation and leadership. They were originally published as a set of papers in early 2008 and since then, the projects featured have moved on. Some have grown and developed, either in collaboration with Oxfam or on their own. They have moved into new areas of work, exploiting opportunities to advance the participation of women in decision-making processes at all levels and in different sectors. Others have altered or scaled back their activities, or even come to an end.

In the broader context, changes in electoral systems, political regimes, and the global economic climate, have presented challenges, as well as new opportunities, to the advancement of women's rights. This chapter provides updates to all the case studies featured in the book (with the exception of Chile as Oxfam GB no longer runs a programme there), as well as a discussion of two important new initiatives: 'Raising Her Voice' is a global programme whose focus in Africa is on supporting the work of the women's movement on the Africa Women's Protocol; 'Women Leading Change in the Middle East and Maghreb region', documents positive examples of women leading in their workplaces and communities.

Updates to the case studies

Chapter 2: Haiti

In Haiti, Fanm Yo La carries on its work of strengthening women's political participation in a climate where women continue to face marginalization and exclusion in the public sphere. The project outlined in the case study has come to an end (as it focused on mobilizing women to participate as candidates and voters in the 2006 elections), but the organization continues to work with Oxfam. Most recently, this has been on the project 'Support for Civil Society Participation and Democratization in Haiti'. As part of this project, an ad hoc 'Haitian advocacy school' was formed. Fanm Yo La and six other national-level civil society organizations attended and were trained in planning strategies, conflict resolution, and networking. Each group then went on to train local level organizations in the methods that they had learned at the advocacy school. As a result, Fanm Yo La provided training to nearly 300 women community leaders. Training covered women's political participation and community leadership, and encouraged them to become involved in civil and political life for the purpose of defending their interests as women. A partnership has also been set up between Fanm Yo La and the Temporary Election Council, to encourage more women to vote in future elections.

Chapter 3: Philippines

The Leadership in Development Programme for Women consisted of a wide range of different activities. These aimed at supporting gender mainstreaming in the programme work of four organizations connected to the fishing industry, and encouraging women in the industry to play a more active role in community-based coastal resource management (CBCRM) and in designing fisheries policy reform.

Since then, Oxfam GB has supported one of the partners, Budyong, to pilot women-only CBCRM projects in which women took over control of the management of resources in three coastal regions. The women fishers initially received training on coastal resources management, and then developed and implemented their own plans to manage their region over the following nine months (supported by Budyong and an external consultant). At the end of this period, participants in the scheme came together to share their experiences.

The pilot scheme was a success, albeit a limited one, given the small scale on which it was run. It has provided a practical example of what happens when women are given priority use rights in coastal areas, and the positive outcomes that this brings. In this instance, these outcomes included improvements in the way that fish stocks and other natural resources such as mangroves were managed, as well as the establishment of a marine sanctuary, and social projects such as film showings and a community pharmacy. In this way, it has placed Budyong in a far stronger position to advocate on behalf of women fishers, strengthening the case for the further integration of their concerns into the National Comprehensive Fisheries Industry Development Plan.[1] It has also improved the leadership and management capacities of the women who took part; this has been recognized by male leaders within the fisher rights movement, who have new-found respect for their female colleagues. Budyong reported that the participants were more self confident, and felt a new-found sense of solidarity with other women fishers, having worked together so closely on the project. The lessons learned from this project, and the work discussed in the case study chapter, are being integrated into other projects around poor women's economic leadership in the Philippines. For instance, another of Oxfam's partners intends to establish a women-managed area within its CBCRM project, as well as making women solely responsible for seaweed processing within its social enterprise project.

Unfortunately, it is uncertain whether Budyong will be able to continue the important work that it has started in promoting the right of women fishers to take an active leadership role in their industry, as changes to Oxfam GB's programme in the Philippines meant that it had to cease funding Budyong earlier than intended. Budyong is at a disadvantage here, for one because it is not clear whether the development of women's leadership is a priority for these advocacy centres, and also because as a relatively 'young' organization, it does not have the track record or experience to be able to 'compete' with some of Oxfam GB's more experienced partners. Budyong is looking elsewhere for funding and technical support to enable it to continue its work, but so far has not succeeded in securing this.

Chapter 4: Cambodia

Since the original publication of the case study, the Female Councillor Forums (FCFs) set up by Women for Prosperity have become entirely self-managing. The forums are now run by women councillors themselves, with official endorsement and financial support from the Ministry of Interior. This is a clear signal that their contribution towards achieving effective decentralized government and gender mainstreaming in planning, budgeting, and social service delivery has been recognized. The FCFs meet three times a year in nine different regions, with up to 300 councillors taking part from across the political spectrum. They continue to provide training and support to women councillors, and opportunities to network and share learning at sessions facilitated by more experienced members.

The fact that this project is continuing without the ongoing support of Oxfam, but with government recognition and support, indicates that it is likely to be sustainable in the long run. This points to the value of incorporating measures to ensure the sustainability of a project beyond its initial funding period and into programme design. In this project, such measures included: informing participants from the very beginning that they would, in time, be taking on responsibility for running the forums; and holding regular workshops with (male) local and national government officials to make sure that they felt involved and came to understand the need for the forums. Another key success of the project has been the building of the confidence and skills of participants – many of whom come from disadvantaged backgrounds – to the extent that they felt ready to take over the management of the FCFs themselves.

Working across party lines, these women councillors have proved themselves to be effective and committed representatives of their constituents, and good political role models. Many have shown particular commitment to the poorest women living in their communities, taking on the responsibility of ensuring that disadvantaged women-headed households have access to adequate housing and income generating projects.

Chapter 5: Sierra Leone

The Women in Leadership (WIL) project run by the 50/50 group and described in the case study has now come to an end, but its successor, Promoting a Culture of Equal Representation (PACER), continues. Elections held in 2007 and 2008 saw the mobilization of over 1,000 women as a result of 50/50's diverse activities. Thirty eight women candidates were directly trained and accompanied by PACER throughout the parliamentary elections in two districts, and nearly 300 potential candidates were trained prior to local elections in Kailahun and Koinadugu districts. Learning from the challenges faced during the WIL project, a special effort was made to identify and engage potential male allies (particularly traditional and religious leaders and former councillors) who would speak out in favour of the right of women to be politically active. Training sessions used specially developed teaching materials, and continued throughout the campaign period. This meant that candidates were far better equipped to run an effective campaign, and to stand up to resistance from their male colleagues and from the electorate. The 50/50 group also worked with local level women's organizations to mobilize support for women candidates.

Fewer women were elected in the 2007 and 2008 elections than the 50/50 Group had hoped, including in the two districts where activities were targeted. There were many reasons for this including changes to the electoral system that meant there was more competition for seats at local government level, and the continued monopoly of male-dominated party politics. But despite this set-back, other outcomes from the project's activities have been very positive. PACER generated a great deal of interest among women wanting to get involved in public life, regardless of whether or not they were elected to office. Indeed, many of the women who were not chosen as candidates, or who stood but were not elected, went on to gain office in other local-level decision-making bodies, such as Ward Development Committees.[2] Others are now working 'behind the scenes' in the offices of women who were elected; many plan to stand for office at the next set of elections. The increased visibility of women candidates and elected officials has also had the effect of encouraging participation at other levels, with more women now attending – and speaking out at – community meetings, and in other forums such as local radio. In this way, the project has helped to strengthen women's leadership and voice at the community level, which is just as important as increasing the number of women present in local and national politics. 50/50 also reports evidence of increased solidarity among women, with female voters now far more willing to support women candidates, seeing them as positive role models and effective legislators.

Chapter 6: UK

Lack of confidence and education; the continued assumption that women are responsible for childcare and reproductive labour within the home; and segregation in the labour market, mean that many women remain trapped in poverty in the UK. This particularly affects those who are raising children on their own. The Voices of Experience and Women's Economic Empowerment projects sought to enable women from disadvantaged backgrounds to meet and lobby the civil servants and politicians who make decisions that impact on their lives, as well as to reflect on their shared experiences of poverty and marginalization.

The projects mentioned in the case study have now come to an end, but the lessons learned from them have gone on to shape the development of Oxfam's work in the UK. The women who participated in the Voices of Experience participatory research project revealed a complex and dynamic understanding of poverty and how it limited their lives, articulating it as an issue of social exclusion and the denial of human rights that went far beyond lack of wealth. This will inform future work, as will reflections on the practical experience of carrying out a participatory research project. These include an appreciation of how important grassroots organizations are in identifying and providing access to research participants, and in supporting them throughout the research process so that they gain from the experience as well. Both this and the Women's Economic Empowerment project brought important insights into the work that needs to go into preparing both participants *and* civil servants and politicians to get the most out of lobbying, such as choosing one topic for lobbying, ensuring that meetings take place on 'neutral ground', and preparing participants for the defensive reactions they may get from local and national officials. They also illustrated how much time and ongoing support women who are not used to having their voices heard need, in order to reach the stage where they are able to articulate their priorities, and advocate for improvements that would make a difference to their lives. The model developed for these projects, combining capacity building, consciousness raising, and enabling participants to lobby policy makers directly, is already being replicated in other Oxfam projects in the UK. The Routes to Solidarity project (working with black and ethnic minority women, who face discrimination not just as a result of their class and gender, but also their ethnicity) and the Gender Works Programme have both benefited from the lessons learned from this model. This project will complement work on poor women's economic leadership, focusing on recognizing and valuing women's unpaid work, and supporting their efforts to secure sustainable incomes.

Chapter 7: Occupied Palestinian Territories and Israel

As discussed in the case study, the active involvement and leadership of Arab Israeli women in popular opposition to the Israeli government's welfare-to-work scheme was a significant and unprecedented move, as was the incorporation of a dedicated Women's Platform into the management structure of Sawt el-Amel. It represented a major shift in gender power relations in this community, where women's presence in the public sphere is often not accepted.

All of Oxfam's activities in Israel and the Occupied Palestinian Territories are now focused on alleviating the poverty and suffering of Palestinians, and Sawt el-Amel's Women's Platform no longer receives support from Oxfam GB. But the Platform now receives funding from Mama Cash,[3] and its activities have gone from strength to strength. These have included: taking legal action on behalf of women against exploitative employers (often just a letter from Sawt el-Amel prompts an employer to hand over unpaid wages); and co-ordinating humanitarian relief during the Israeli bombardment of Gaza in 2008. The Women's Platform has now turned its attention inwards to concentrate on putting a clear and transparent leadership structure in place and developing a strategic plan, whilst also strengthening the skills and capacities of the dedicated activists within the group.

Chapter 8: Honduras

The project described in the case study saw important links established between women's rights organizations and women elected to Congress. Since then, these relationships have been nurtured and now form the focus of Visitacíon Padilla's work, along with continued lobbying for the country's political parties to respect the 30 per cent quota for female candidates introduced as part of electoral reform prior to the 2005 elections.

The outcomes of these activities have been mixed. In elections held at the end of 2008, the 30 per cent quota was widely flouted by the main parties. They got round the law by including women candidates in their lists as alternates, rather than full candidates. As this is in breach of electoral law, Visitacíon Padilla has taken the case to the Supreme Electoral Court, and will go on to take the case up to the Supreme Court of Justice and the Inter-American Court of Human Rights if necessary. There have also been few advances in the approval and implementation of pro-poor and pro-women's rights policies in Congress or the Senate.

On a more positive note, while the main parties are ignoring the 30 per cent quota, it was adopted by all the minority parties at the 2008 elections. While this has not resulted in a significant increase in the number of women elected, it is a positive and important step. Visitacíon Padilla's training and lobbying of congresswomen – particularly those allied to the majority conservative party – has also paid off. A 'women's bloc' in congress has formed to press for the electoral quota for women candidates to be raised from 30 to 50 per cent. It is also pressing for the investigation of high levels of femicide[4] in Honduras, and trying to counter attempts made by other policy makers to restrict women's rights. In this regard, women's rights organizations were successful in lobbying the bloc to oppose an amendment suggested by conservative law-makers to ban the import, distribution, and use of emergency contraceptive pills; as a result, the ban was not imposed.

New Initiatives

Raising Her Voice

Launched in August 2008 and initiated and managed by Oxfam GB, the overall objective of the five year 'Raising Her Voice' (RHV)[5] project is to promote the rights and capacities of poor women to engage effectively in governance at all levels, by ensuring that public policy, decision-making, and expenditure reflect the interests of poor and marginalized women, especially those excluded from political, social, and economic life. In this way, it aims to show how bringing poor women's voices into processes of governance, as well as improving those processes to make them more responsive and accountable, can have a positive impact on the lives of people living in poverty. The programme addresses the general obstacles to women's engagement in governance, as well as the specific obstacles faced by particular groups of women in particular places.

Ensuring women's active participation and leadership is key to the achieve-ment of this objective, particularly within civil-society organizations that are in a position to influence changes in governing policies and practices, and to hold governments and other decision-making bodies to account. But wom-en's leadership *within* those decision-making bodies is also important. This is because a 'critical mass' of women policy makers actively committed to gender equality will boost the capacity of these institutions to recognize and act on their obligations and commitments to address women's rights, as well as meaning that gender-sensitive legislation is more likely to be put in place and implemented. In doing so, these activities illustrate the range of ways that women's leadership can interact with governance at many different levels, as well as the importance of making links between local, regional, national, and global leadership initiatives.

RHV covers 19 projects across a wide geographical area. These include ac-tivities in Indonesia, Nepal, Pakistan, Bolivia, Chile (managed from Bolivia, as Oxfam no longer has an office in Chile), Guatemala, Honduras, Albania, and Armenia. In Africa, it includes a Pan-African regional co-ordination proj-ect, and eight national level projects. These projects are campaigning for the ratification of the Africa Women's Protocol in Sudan and Uganda, and for the integration of the Protocol's articles into national legislation in The Gambia, Liberia, Mozambique, Nigeria, South Africa, and Tanzania (all of which have already ratified the Protocol).

Global activities

In Nepal, the project uses radio to reach women living in rural areas, and en-courage them to take part in advocacy and campaigning on women's rights in governance and conflict mitigation. In addition, partner organizations are supporting women standing for government office, and those who are elected, with the aim of increasing political participation at all levels. Work in Pakistan focuses on government accountability and budget monitoring. In Indonesia, it aims to ensure that poor women benefit from community-level development planning led by state and traditional governance institutions.

Project work in Bolivia, Chile, Guatemala, and Honduras aims to enable women from poor and marginalized communities to be 'proactive' citizens, aware of their rights and contributing to decision-making processes. In Bolivia, Oxfam's partners are working with women from poor urban districts; in Chile, with migrant women workers to design and press for new legislation protecting their rights, and also with women elected to office to encourage them to advocate within government for the rights of poor and marginalized women. Rural and indigenous women in Guatemala and Honduras face particular hardship and exclusion: in both countries, project work focuses on supporting their leadership within their communities, and on linking this local activism with national civil-society organizations and their activities.

Rural women in Albania also face isolation and marginalization. There, partners are working to increase their participation in rural development planning, through innovative partnerships between civil-society organizations, state institutions, and the private sector. In Armenia, disabled women are particularly marginalized; here activities are concentrated on bringing such women's voices into local government decision-making processes, in the context of improving the quality of, and access to, services for people with disabilities.

Africa Women's Protocol

RHV activities in the eight African countries centre around the ratification and implementation of the African Union's 'Protocol to the African Charter on Human and People's Rights on the Rights of Women in Africa', known as the Africa Women's Protocol.[6] The Protocol came into force in 2005, and is the only regional treaty that provides mechanisms for the protection of women's rights in the continent in line with international policy frameworks (such as CEDAW, the MDGs, and the UDHR).[7]

The Protocol also contains articles relating to issues that particularly affect women living across Africa, such as HIV and AIDS, trafficking, and traditional practices such as female genital mutilation (FGM), widow inheritance, and property grabbing.[8] Significantly, it is also the first legally binding human rights instrument to recognize women's reproductive rights as human rights. In this regard, the Protocol reaffirms principles set out in earlier documents relating to maternal health, family planning, and HIV prevention, but also commits states to the legalisation of abortion in cases of rape, incest, sexual violence, and/or where a woman's life would be endangered as a result of continuing her pregnancy. Articles compelling states to eradicate sexual and gender-based violence are included; one article directs states to treat sexual violence directed at women during armed conflict as a war crime and a genocidal act. The Protocol reinforces women's rights to dignity, integrity, respect, and security, and is a vital tool by which women's rights organizations within the countries that have ratified can lobby their governments to draw up and implement legislation protecting and upholding women's rights.

Since the Protocol's adoption in 2003, Oxfam has been involved in the Pan-African campaign to encourage its ratification, domestication, and implementation, as part of the Solidarity for African Women's Rights (SOAWR) coalition.[9] Thanks to an innovative campaign by SOAWR,[10] the Protocol came into force in November 2005 with Togo's ratification, the 15th country to do so.

Since then, SOAWR's endeavours have moved to campaigning for national governments to integrate the provisions of the Protocol into national law, and to raise awareness of the Protocol and the rights that it enshrines, particularly among women from rural, poor, and otherwise marginalized communities. RHV will provide support to these activities in The Gambia, Liberia, Mozambique, Nigeria, South Africa, Sudan, Tanzania, and Uganda until 2013. In the process, this will strengthen the advocacy and campaigning capacities of the national member organizations of SOAWR and help to ensure that the campaign does not lose momentum. Recent work has included meetings to raise awareness of the Protocol in Liberia; a march on International Women's Day (8 March) in Mozambique to press the government to pass the domestic violence bill (which integrates the articles in the Protocol on violence against women); and awareness raising in the media on the provisions relating to FGM in Tanzania. In Uganda, lobbying for ratification continues. Across the region, many activities have focused on breaking down the provisions in the Protocol and explaining what they mean to people who are not used to reading complex legal documents, meaning that they can then see how the provisions relate to their own lives.

At the regional level, SOAWR is working with the African Union and the United Nations Development Fund for Women (UNIFEM) to convene a regional conference to discuss the implementation of the Protocol and the integration of its provisions into national law in the countries that have ratified. SOAWR has also recently published a book *Advocating for Women's Rights: Experiences from Solidarity for African Women's Rights Coalition*, and joined Oxfam International in hosting a session at the 2009 CSW.[11] This provided an opportunity for women leaders and community activists to speak on behalf of poor and marginalized women affected by HIV and AIDS about the obstacles they face, and the progress made in realizing their rights, as enshrined in the Protocol.

Given that most countries are still going through the process of integrating the provisions of the Protocol into domestic law, it is still too early to say what final impact the Protocol will have in terms of improving the lives of women in the countries that have ratified. That said, the Protocol has been cited in some very significant developments. Rwanda and South Africa were two of the earliest countries to ratify; both subsequently went on to legislate – and implement – 50 per cent quotas for women at national and local level govern- ment respectively. There is great potential for this campaigning force to be mobilized to advocate women's rights and gender equality in other areas, such as financial institutions in the wake of the current global economic downturn, or those bodies set up to mitigate the effects of climate change.

Women Leading Change in the Middle East and Maghreb region

The Women Leading Change in the Middle East and Maghreb region project forms part of Oxfam International's work on gender justice, and draws together work on women's leadership in this region carried out by several of the Oxfam affiliates and their partners.[12] Through providing positive examples of women assuming leadership positions, the scheme aims to promote women in the re- gion as actors for positive change and to challenge negative stereotypes. In this way, it is hoped that other women across the region – particularly those who are marginalized as a result of poverty or other forms of social exclusion – will be inspired to take up leadership positions themselves in their households, com- munities and workplaces, and will benefit from improved control over their own lives. It is also hoped that they will benefit from other women leaders who are realizing their commitment to furthering the rights, concerns, and opportu- nities of women and girls living in poverty.

The project began fairly recently in 2008, with the collation of eight case studies. These were based on interviews with representatives of partner orga- nizations, giving the women who participated an important opportunity to voice their own thoughts on the work that they were doing and how it con- tributed to improving the lives of other women. The case studies covered the following projects:

- Small loans and support to women entrepreneurs, Occupied Palestinian Territories
- Strengthening community champions against FGM, Egypt
- Counselling and reception centres for women victims of violence, Morocco
- Support for single mothers, and revenue generating enterprises, Morocco
- Building capacity of local women's organizations to provide legal and social services, Occupied Palestinian Territories
- Organizing women workers, Egypt
- Legal support and protection programme, Yemen
- Integrating a gender approach into the national development plan, Yemen

Members of the different partner organizations involved then came together in November 2008 for a three-day workshop. During this session, they reflected on the impact of their activities, and how they represented progressive, trans- formative leadership. They concluded the following:

1. By offering services such as shelter to victims of violence, legal advice, and acting as role models, they were helping other women to take control over their own lives.
2. By expanding their actions beyond their own organizations – working with people in the community and identifying community champions, supporting smaller civil society organizations, engaging with state institutions and with national government to hold them to account – they were acting as a bridge between local people and the institutions that impact on their lives, helping to ensure that their voices are heard.
3. By speaking out about sensitive issues such as gender-based violence they were raising awareness, and helping women and girls affected to realize that they are not alone, and can seek help.
4. By talking to people about gender issues and women's rights in an open, non-confrontational way – listening to their views, using arguments that encourage rather than scare, and examples that point to the mutual benefits of upholding women's rights – they were succeeding in changing deep-seated negative stereotypes about gender roles and relations.

The project is still in its early stages. It is hoped that it will eventually lead to the creation of a bank of positive, personal stories of women bringing about change in the Middle East and Maghreb, which will be used to inform policy and programme work, as well as providing inspiration to other women within the region and beyond.

About the author

Joanna Hoare wrote this chapter while working for Oxfam GB. She now works as a freelance editor and writer on gender and development issues.

References

Izumi, Kaori (2007) 'Gender-based violence and property grabbing in Africa: a denial of women's liberty and security', *Gender & Development*, 15:1, pp. 11-23

Oxfam GB (2008) 'Policy, advocacy and programming on the Africa Women's Protocol: overview of Oxfam GB's support to women's-rights organizations and government stakeholders in Southern Africa', Programme Insights: Southern Africa, Oxford: Oxfam

Prieto-Carrón, Marina, Thomson, Marilyn, and Macdonald, Mandy (2007) 'No more killings! Women respond to femicides in Central America', *Gender & Development*, 15:1, pp. 25-40

Notes

1. This is the main piece of legislation relating to the fishing industry in the Philippines.

2. Ward Development Committees are the lowest level of local government, and provide a vital link between communities and local councils.
3. Mama Cash is an international foundation which exclusively funds women's rights projects. www.mamacash.org (last accessed June 2009).
4. 'Femicide' ('femicidio' or 'feminicidio' in Spanish) refers to the violent murder of women. Central America and Mexico have seen an alarming rise in the number of women killed violently since the mid-1990s, and the term has come to be used by women's rights groups in the region 'as a legal and political term to refer to the murder of women killed *because they are women*' (Prieto-Carrón, Thomson, and Macdonald, 2007: 25).
5. RHV is co-funded by the UK Department for International Development (DfID) under the Global Transparency Fund, and United Nations Development Programme (UNDP).
6. To read the full text of the Protocol, please visit www.achpr.org/english/_ info/women_en.html (last accessed June 2009).
7. Convention on the Elimination of All forms of Discrimination against women (CEDAW), Millennium Development Goals (MDGs), Universal Declaration of Human Rights (UDHR).
8. Property grabbing relates to the practice of relatives of a deceased man 'grabbing' property that should rightfully belong to his widow and children (Izumi 2007)
9. The members of SOAWR are: Equality Now, Kenya; Africa Centre for Democracy and Human Rights Studies, The Gambia; Women of Liberia Peace Network, Liberia; Women's Non Governmental Organizations Secretariat of Liberia; Forum Mulher, Mozambique; Women's Rights Advancement and Protection Alternative, Nigeria; People Opposing Women Abuse, South Africa; Strategic Initiative for Women in the Horn of Africa, Sudan; Legal and Human Rights Centre, Tanzania; Akina Mama wa Afrika, Uganda, and Oxfam GB.
10. For information about this campaign, please see Caroline Muthoni Muriithi writing in Pambazuka News: http://www.pambazuka.org/en/category/comment/44597 (last accessed June 2009).
11. The Commission on the Status of Women (CSW) is held every year at UN Headquarters in New York. Representatives from UN member states gather together to evaluate global progress towards achieving gender equality. It is an important opportunity for women's rights activists to lobby for legislative changes at the national and international level. For more information, see http://www.un.org/womenwatch/daw/csw/ (last accessed June 2009).
12. Oxfam International is a confederation of thirteen organizations working together in more than 100 countries to find lasting solutions to poverty and injustice. Oxfam GB is one of the thirteen affiliates.

Index